THE CULTURAL HISTORY OF
SPAIN

THE CULTURAL HISTORY OF
SPAIN

TEXT AND PHOTOGRAPHS
BY HENRI STIERLIN

Cover

This majestic representation of Christ decorating Saint Clement's Church at Tahull is one of the high points of monumental Romanesque painting.

Endpapers

The Roman aqueduct at Segovia, built in the time of Trajan in the early second century AD, is over 800 metres (870 yards) long and stands 30 metres (100 feet) above the small valley it was built to span. Its hundred and twenty-eight arches still carry a conduit bringing water to the city.

Title page

With her grave air and her soft and mysterious gaze, the "Lady of Elche" is the most famous sculpture in Spain from the Hellenised Iberian culture. Dating from the fifth or fourth century BC, this work symbolises the great mother goddess, the Tanit-Astarte of the Phœnicians, and must have served both as a cinerary urn and as a viaticum for the journey to the next world in the tomb of an important man. She wears rich jewellery and must have been painted in colour.

Photo credits

The 155 colour photographs which illustrate this volume are all the work of Henri Stierlin, with the following exceptions:
André Corboz, Zurich, pages 33-35, 42, 44-45.
Maurice Babey, Bâle (Ziolo), pages 43 and 74.
Oroñoz, Madrid (Ziolo), pages 67, 75 and 91 left.
The author and photographer would like to express his gratitude to the Spanish authorities for their help in his work, and in particular to thank Mr. Luis Miravitlles, General Director of Tourism, Madame Soledad Diez-Picazo, Directress of the Spanish National Tourist Office in Geneva, the management of the National Archaeological Museum in Madrid and of the Museum of Catalan Art in Barcelona, and the management of the National Library in Madrid and of the Royal Library at Escorial.

© *Agence Internationale d'Edition*
Jean-François Gonthier,
1009 Pully (Switzerland), 1982.
This edition: Edito-Service S.A., Geneva,
(Switzerland), 1983.
Translated by Harriet Coleman.

ISBN 2-8302-0611-8
13 089 011

Printed in Italy

Contents

Before the Dawn of History

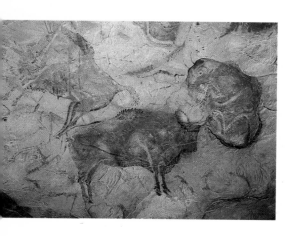

Part of the painted ceiling in the cave at Altamira: the high point of Palaeolithic cave art, painted some fifteeen thousand years ago, it is composed mainly of bison in red ochre, iron oxide and charcoal.

In this "Cultural History of Spain" we offer an overview of the works of art and treasures it seemed legitimate to include in a volume devoted to the Iberian peninsula. In fact, because of its geographical and historical situation, this region constitutes a world apart. It is not a question of excluding Spain from the community of Europe but rather of underlining the particularity of its history, the better to understand what has made up the originality of its art.

Well over twice the size of the United Kingdom, the Iberian peninsula is isolated from the rest of Europe by the high barrier of the Pyrenees, and from North Africa by the Straits of Gibraltar, meeting point of the Mediterranean and the Atlantic. But here at the Western extremity of Europe its situation makes it at the same time a bridge between Europe and Africa, and it is this fact that has governed its whole history; for Spain has swung like a pendulum through history, now a living part of the European continent, now closer to African developments. Between these two extremes there have been periods, too, of isolationism, when Spain has turned in on itself.

Emerging from prehistory, the peninsula became solidly tied to the great trading and maritime power of the Carthaginians, who founded their city of Cartagena in Spain, a counterpart to Carthage, city of Phœnician origin on the North African coast. Spain was thus integrated with the southern coast of the Mediterranean. But once the adventure of the Punic Wars was over, it became part of the Roman Empire, and remained one of its brightest jewels for five hundred years.

Then the great invasions dismantled the Roman empire. Spain was soon reunited—at the end of the 5th century—under the leadership of the Visigothic kings of Toledo, though during the same period Europe beyond the Pyrenees was ravaged and torn to pieces by plundering hordes of invaders. Unity under the Visigoths, however was forged only at the price of accepting the Toledan kings' Arian heresy, and Arianism cut the country off from the rest of Europe, which was Catholic. When the court finally embraced the faith of the people, the Isidorian renaissance in the 7th century bathed Spain in the glow of a culture unknown, at that early date, to the rest of Europe.

But with the collapse of the Visigothic kingdom before the Berbers and Arabs, the outcome was again quite particular to Spain. Between 711 and 714 the whole country was absorbed as a province of the Moslem world, and the pendulum swung back towards Africa. During the seven hundred years that followed, Moorish culture gave Spain an appearance unique among Western countries. Here flourished a high culture, a syncretic culture drawing in the most diverse currents: Arab (Umayyad), Christian Mozarab, Byzantine, Berber, Jewish.

Through the ups and downs of the Reconquista, led by the kingdoms of Asturia and Leon, one may see the development among the Christians of northern Spain of a specific nationalism, founded also on the Mozarab rite. But the rest of Europe, strengthened by the rise of the great monastic orders, set out implacably to crush this specifically Hispanic development, and pulled Spain into the orbit of Catholicism. The task was carried out by the Emperor and the Papacy, with the help of priests from France and Italy and the influence of the Pilgrims of St. James during the Romanesque and Gothic periods.

The end of the Reconquista, with the fall of Granada in 1492, the same year as the discovery of the New World, marks a major mile-stone for Spain: turning towards colonial expansion, the country was to follow a different path from those other European countries whose overseas conquests began at a later date. Spain thus pulled itself up to the head of the nations of the West. In the 16th century, with the establishment of an empire on which the sun never set, Spain stamped its indelible imprint across the whole globe, as the two hundred million Spanish-speakers across the world today bear witness.

This brief glimpse, then, shows the specificity of Spanish history and of the arts that blossomed in the peninsula—welded for a while to the fate of the West, for a while to that of North Africa and the Middle East—a specificity that fully justifies the dedication of a full volume in our series to "The Cultural History of Spain".

Detail of a bison from Altamira. The stone age artists have given both elegance and power to the big beast that constituted the essential basis of their subsistence (National Archaeological Museum, Madrid).

The richness of Spain

This study, then, delving into Spain's past, will begin with art works fifteen thousand years old, the New Stone Age cave paintings of Altamira. It will lead us through the prehistoric, Phœnician, Ibero-

Celtic, Graeco-Roman, Visigothic, Arab and Asturian periods up to the flowering of the Romanesque and Gothic ages and to that rich Renaissance which gave the country the great epic of the Conquistadors. It will end with a brief evocation of the age of the Baroque. It is a synthetic and eclectic glimpse: the richness of Spain's heritage in art and architecture makes our choice necessarily partial. It would be easy enough to point out the gaps in our presentation; we have, however, included the most varied aspects of the art of Spain and its different provinces, from Catalonia to Andalusia, from Castile to Asturia and Galicia, embracing Madrid and Toledo, Granada and Cordova, Barcelona, Avila, Segovia, Oviedo and Leon.

The wealth of Spain's museums is exemplary: for instance the remarkable Archaeological Museum in Madrid, recently and most successfully re-arranged in a fresh presentation, or the medieval collection in the Museum of Catalan Art in Barcelona bringing together the most extraordinary ensemble of Romanesque paintings imaginable. As to the magnificent library collections—in the Escorial and the National Library in Madrid—they can be evoked only by one or another of their sumptuous illuminated manuscripts, so numerous both from the Mozarab-Romanesque period and from the Gothic.

Like the other titles in the series, this "Cultural History of Spain" sets out to evoke the country's archaeological and monumental riches. It is these we have mainly dealt with, whatever the importance of Spanish painting, with the brilliance of El Greco, Velasquez and Goya. For it is these architectural works, sculptures and the so-called "minor arts"— ivories, bronzes, goldsmiths' work, etc—which are less often the subject of publications.

Scouting Spain for the illustrative material for this volume we became conscious of the wealth of this country's heritage and the innumerable works which still remain little known to the tourists who head, all too often, straight for the beach, while the interior of the country is little visited except for the tourist centres of Granada, Cordova and Seville.

Fifteen thousand years ago

We have to go back fifteen thousand years to discover the peninsula's first great artistic inheritance: the cave paintings of Altamira, dating from the Upper Palaeolithic age (Solutrian and Magdalenian). In fact, carbon 14 analysis dates the Old Magdalenian period, the period of the finest works at Altamira, at around 13,500 BC.

The story of the discovery of this holy of holies of Palaeolithic art, which has been called the "Sistine Chapel of prehistory", is a real fairy-tale. In 1879 the archaeologist de Santuola took his small daughter with him into the caves in the Cantabrian mountains near Santillana del Mar, in the province of Santander. Inside, she looked up, and cried out in

The Cueva de Menga near Antequera is one of the biggest dolmens in all the megalithic architecture of Europe. This view from the end of the hall towards the entrance shows the imposing blocks of stone that make up the walls and roof of the building.

surprise on seeing the outlines of animals on the roof of the cave. Her
father had been more preoccupied by the remains buried in the earth
floor than by the walls of the great cavern, and had noticed nothing. He
met with nothing but scepticism from the outside world, and when he
claimed that these paintings of bison and horses, ibex and stags were
several thousand years old, he was even regarded as the author of a joke
in bad taste, if not a mystification or a fraud.

In 1902 the Abbot Breuil made one of his first scientific surveys at
Altamira and made a serious attempt to establish the date of the
paintings within the Palaeolithic age. Some 250 metres (820 feet) long
and decorated throughout with these paintings, the cave has, in particular, 25 metres (82 feet) to the left of the entrance, a side passage, 18
metres long by 9 wide (60 feet by 30), its ceiling covered with magnificent
paintings. Here stone age art attains one of its high points, to which
only Lascaux and Niaux in France can be compared.

*Held up by three large pillars down the
centre, the ceiling slabs of the Cueva de
Menga and the walls of this great burial
chamber built around 2500 BC may
weigh up to 180 tons.*

The great hall of the Cueva del Romeral, a truncated conical structure built in dry stone with small cut blocks and closed off at the top by an enormous slab of rock. This is the building technology of 1800 BC. At the far end, the small funerary chamber.

Top:
The half-collapsed entrance to the tumulus of the Cueva del Romeral, near Antequera. The dolmen's passageway has almost entirely disappeared, but it was built of megalithic slabs forming a trapezoidal portico.

The new stone age tribes must have celebrated their propitiatory rites here before the hunting expeditions on which the survival of their families depended. For generations the "painter-shamans" must endlessly have followed the same themes; for the outlines of animals leap over each other and sometimes overlap in an inextricable, colourful "palimpsest" throughout the length of the cave.

Be that as it may, the qualities of the artistic expression achieved by the "artist-sorcerers" of Altamira combine an exceptional sense of observation of wild animals with an expressionism that accentuates particular characteristics of each species. In particular, the bulk of the body is greatly exaggerated in relation to the legs, as if to designate for the kill good fat beasts with plenty of flesh and hence plentiful nourishment. So bisons and horses become essentially a mass of meat on slender legs — though this does not detract from the power and elegance of the paintings.

It is true that one great prehistorian, André Leroi-Gourhan, has contested this theory of cave painting as a ritual aid to the hunt. He sees it as a symbolic association of the various species, somewhat like a holy painting: the cave would thus be a great sanctuary decorated for some complex ritual, perhaps comparable to a kind of passage through the stations of the cross in the prehistoric religion. Though we have lost the key to this symbolism, its composition remains the same from one cave to another throughout Franco-Cantabrian cave painting.

Northern Spain thus seems to have constituted, in this distant age of the Upper Palaeolithic, an entity closely associated with the Perigord region; and the links are many, too, with the art of the Dordogne caves.

From the Neolithic to the bronze age

A few thousand years later, at the end of the Mesolithic and the dawn of the Neolithic age (between 6000 and 4000 BC), this cave art underwent profound changes, as witness the rock paintings of eastern Spain. Instead of finding almost exclusively the painted figures of animals, here the principal iconographic themes are above all human figures—hunters with their bows, dancers, honey-gatherers and so on. These paintings—which are, sadly, very poorly preserved—may be related to those in the Sahara, found under the shelter of certain rocks. If this is so, the alternation of the poles of attraction acting on Spain would be established right from pre-history on, relations with what is today central France being followed by the establishment of contact with the populations of northern Africa, where the Sahara, in the process of drying up, still had enough water to provide grazing on its steppes for herds of elephant, hippopotamus, giraffe, gazelle, and possibly even the earliest flocks of domesticated cattle.

For the great revolution which made the New Stone Age was characterised in its initial phase by the domestication first of small livestock, then of large. In the place of the food-gathering and hunting tribes of the flaked-stone period there emerged populations who made their livelihood from a pastoral economy. The New Stone Age proper, however, is characterised by the development of the cultivation of crops. The earliest evidence of this comes from 10,000 BC in the Middle East, from where it had progressively conquered the whole of the Fertile Crescent by 5000 BC.

Between, 4000 and 3000 BC the cultivators expanded across Europe from east to west, along the Danube plains on the one hand and by the sea routes of the Mediterranean on the other. So it was that agriculture reached the eastern coast of Spain around 3300 BC.

Going hand in hand with the sedentarisation of the population and with a population growth that followed on from the increase in the food supply, agriculture was generally followed in turn by the invention of pottery. In the social field, this same evolution led to the appearance of the first villages, fortified by earthworks to protect both the families and the herds and granaries inevitably coveted by outsiders.

But while this diffusion of agricultural techniques was developing through a step-by-step transmission of particular skills that had sprung up in the Middle East, the same process was going on in another domaine—that of religious ideas and beliefs. It seems to have been in this way that, through a second migratory wave of populations more advanced than the farmers of the western Mediterranean, a new religion was disseminated, characterised by its huge stone constructions, generally for funerary purposes, known as megaliths.

This megalithic religion seems to constitute the first great missionary movement to have unfolded along the coasts of Europe, coming first from the Near East. Certainly there is still debate over the relation between the dolmens of the Caucasus, the Greek tholoï, the temples of Malta, the megalithic tombs of Sicily and the nourraghes of Sardinia. But it remains the case that the wave which reached from the southern coast of Spain and Portugal as far as Brittany, Ireland, England and Scotland, to reach the Danish and Scandinavian coasts during the Bronze Age, must demonstrate the existence of a veritable "proselytism".

In southern Spain, in the province of Malaga, and more precisely at Antequera, a city overlooking the rich plain onto which one emerges after crossing over the Sierra de Torcales from the sea, stands one of the most remarkable of these Spanish megalithic monuments: the Cueva de Menga. It is a funerary tumulus dating back to 2500 years before the

Three examples of prehistoric art from the Spanish bronze age. Top, the stele-idol from Hernan Perez in Cáceres province, representing a solar god; left, the funerary stele from Solana de Cabanas, also in Cáceres province, showing a chariot tomb burial with weapons, shield and four-wheeled war chariot beside a dead warrior; and on the right, a small cylindrical idol in alabaster, from Estremadura, and representing a solar deity (National Archaeological Museum, Madrid).

11

birth of Christ—earlier than the great Pyramids of Egypt. This huge construction, fruit of the collective effort of a whole population of the late Neolithic age, contains a vast oval chamber 25 metres (82 feet) long, oriented east to west, walled by formidable upright stone slabs. In the centre of the hall is an alignment of three powerful stone pillars supporting the flat roof, itself made of gigantic stone slabs, the largest of which is 7 metres (23 feet) across and must weigh some 180 tons.

If one studies these great rock slabs, apparently barely roughcut, one can see that while the visible surfaces have been left almost in their raw state, the faces between two slabs are admirably jointed. Despite the huge size of the stone blocks used, the joints between the wall slabs and between these and the ceiling slabs are of an astonishing precision. Grooves have been cut out to keep the whole together and prevent any displacement under pressure of the mass of earth—several hundred tons of it—built up to form the tumulus around and over the megalithic structure, hiding it completely.

One of the biggest dolmens in Europe, and a magnificent example of pre-historic architecture, the Cueva de Menga proves that its builders possessed a remarkable science and technology—and were, in addition, motivated by an intense collective faith in gods of whom, unfortunately, we know nothing at all.

The Antequera site also offers another such prehistoric funerary construction covered by a tumulus: this is the Cueva del Romeral. It is a later work, and must date from 1900 to 1800 BC; here the only megalithic elements are the trapezoid entrance gallery, 20 metres (65 feet) long and partly in ruins, and the slab over the central chamber. In

With the same wheels for eyes as the alabaster idol on the previous page, this idol carved on a slate plaque goes back to the megalithic period and was discovered in Estremadura (National Archaeological Museum, Madrid).

Bell-shaped ceramic from the Bronze Age, with a decoration incised and applied in white slip, from Ciempozuelos, near Madrid. This container, furnished with a lid, is in black clay and dates back to the second millenium BC (National Archaeological Museum, Madrid).

fact the constructions of the period are henceforth circular dry-stone chambers of small cut stone blocks, rising in a conical "false vault" but closed over at the top by one flat monolith. Behind this first chamber a smaller hall, also circular, forms as it were a chapel. The Cueva del Romeral is one of the earliest examples of dressed-stone architecture we know of in Western Europe.

Whatever may be said of the megalithic constructions built by the Iberians, one cannot but admire the tenacity and collective effort which must have gone into the transport, often across dozens of miles, of these huge blocks of stone, hauled on rollers or on beds of clay by men harnessed to ropes as thick as a man's arm.

Certain works dating from the very end of the megalithic period are also decorated with carvings, as for example in the case of the steles of southern Spain which show what may be a solar god.

The invention of metalworking

This megalithic culture stretches as far as the turning point between the age of polished stone, the Chalcolithic (or Copper Age) civilisation, and the Bronze Age. The introduction of metalworking, however, was to revolutionise technology only when the use of bronze for tools became generalised, which in Spain seems to have been around 1500 BC.

Between 2000 and 1000 BC one observes the presence in Spain of curious cylindrical idols with an anthropomorphic decoration in which the eyes are represented by solar wheels. The same eyes in the form of wheels appear on carved slate plaques also dating from the Bronze Age.

But the protohistoric find which has the richest lessons for us is perhaps the funerary slab found at Solana de Cabanas, near Logrosan in the province of Cáceres. This slab, which once roofed a burial chamber, bears a decoration showing, from top to bottom, a wide-pointed lance, a flat sword typical of the late Bronze Age, a mirror and a helmet, and, below to the left, a great shield with indented sides, to the right of which lies a dead warrior; at the bottom one can distinguish a four-wheeled war chariot. These various items are arranged like the furnishings of a tomb. They are informative on the one hand about the weapons of the time (around 1000 BC), and on the other hand about the burial customs for warriors. The carving is in fact evocative of chariot tombs, with the chariot here replaced by a simple graphic representation. We know that such chariot tombs were in use across a considerable area, stretching from Siberia and China to the Atlantic. Examples are found dating up to 500 BC, as for example in the Celtic tomb at Vix in Burgundy.

An odd similarity of decoration connects two works we reproduce here: on the one hand a bell-shaped black pottery vase with a cross motif, incised and embossed in white slip, its style seeming to be inspired by carved wooden vessels (this work may date back to 1500-1000 BC), and on the other hand a much later piece: the curious solid gold cup from Axtroki in the Basque country, where besides the similar cruciform decoration there are concentric circles and Celtic-styles repoussé work

A fine example of Celtic goldwork in Spain: this double torc with its incised decoration and an ingenious clasp at the back was found, together with the bracelets, at Sagrajas in Cáceres province (National Archaeological Museum, Madrid).

An elegant Celtic bracelet in gold; it is square in cross section (National Archaeological Museum, Madrid).

imitating granulations. There seems thus to have existed, beyond the divisions of historical periods, a heritage and a filiation defining the distinctive traits of a specific artistic current.

This brings us to the story of that strange migratory people, the Celts, who around the 8th century BC, at the end of the Hallstatt period, reached Spanish territory where they were to retain a presence throughout the La Teine period (from 500 BC up to the first affirmation of the Roman empire). The Celts, originating in central Europe, occupied an important place in Spain, alongside the Iberians, with whom they soon mixed to produce what is known as the Celtiberian culture.

The Celts spread not only as far as Estremadura but in other directions as far as Rome, Greece, Asia Minor and southern Russia. Warlike and unstable, they produced above all an interesting craft in goldwork. Their favourite decorations were torcs, tubular metal collars which we see appear in womens' tombs from the 5th century BC on. Made of gold or silver, these torcs and the bracelets made in the same very simple style bear witness to a real virtuosity in the art of metalwork, and to a deep

Celtic torc in twisted silver, from the Carrion river basin in Palencia province. Silver is a metal rarely used by the Celts, and the style of the work too shows the influence of Classical art (National Archaeological Museum, Madrid).

sensitivity to the materials used, always soberly decorated.

Finally certain Celtic coronets found in northern Spain show a whole iconography in which horsemen mingle with figures beside great cauldrons (irresistibly reminiscent of the famous vase of Vix!). These works probably tell a mythical story from the Celtic epic.

A melting-pot...

This long period of pre-history thus first shows the multiple influences acting on the country, coming from the East, from central Europe and from Africa. This aspect of Spain as a meeting-point of cultures is to be accentuated at the dawn of history, demonstrating in the most striking way that this far end of the Eurasian continent, far from being first and foremost a cul-de-sac as one might think, has been, on the contrary, a melting-pot of peoples, ideas, varied styles and currents, from which it has created the very substance of its own culture.

Left:
Gold cup from the late Bronze Age, from Axtroki in the Basque country. In a purely Celtic design, repoussé work in imitation of granulated work introduces a foreign element, perhaps the influence of Etruscan tendencies (National Archaeological Museum, Madrid).

Detail of a fragment from a gold coronet found at Cangas de Onis in the province of Oviedo. A scene with horsemen and other human figures in repoussée work, with large cauldrons which must have played an important rôle in Celtic mythology (National Archaeological Museum, Madrid).

The Classical Arts in Spain

Bronze statuette of Phœnician origin, discovered in Cadiz, showing a deity in the classic pose of the god Ptah of Pharaonic Egyptian art. A gold mask covers his face, showing that «gold is the flesh of the gods». This piece, 13 centimetres (5 inches) high, must date back to the eighth century BC (National Archaeological Museum, Madrid).

The entry of the Iberians into the community of historical cultures, that is to say those with writing, took place under the two-fold influence of the Phœnicians and their successors the Carthaginians on the one hand, and of the Greeks on the other, more particularly the colonies founded by the Ionian Greek city of Phocaea. It was thus the concurrent contributions of two currents from the eastern Mediterranean arriving on the east coast of Spain that brought the land of Iberia into history by giving it the alphabet. The script of the Iberians was in fact inspired by that of the Phœnicians, with certain forms adopted from the Greek, thouth we should not forget that the Greek alphabet was itself derived from the Phœnician.

But this civilising movement remained for a while restricted to the southern and eastern coasts of the peninsula. Greek and Phœnician influences penetrated only slowly: the centre and north of the country remained purely Celtiberian right up to the Roman conquest. The ports established by the Greeks and Phœnicians, basically trading posts, hardly sought to become colonies in the true sense, and had therefore only a slight influence on the interior of the country during the first centuries of their implantation.

These foreign bases on Spanish soil restricted themselves to establishing commercial movements right across the peninsula, providing in this way an outlet for the country's ores and produce so sought after by the merchants of the East. So a fruitful exchange with the Celtiberians was born. The indigenous population furnished the Orient with tin, an indispensible component of bronze, first of all mining it on Spanish soil and later, unable themselves to meet the growing demand, importing it from their neighbours to the north. Perhaps their supplies were augmented by the fleet of the Veneti, a Celtic people from Brittany who brought provisions from the far-off Cassiterid isles, the Scilly isles of today, off the south-west coast of Britain. In exchange, the Celtiberians acquired luxury goods and ornaments, ceramics and eastern perfumes. For them as for the Celtic tribes of the Rhone valley, the outcome was a developing contact with the products of high civilisations whose creations now entered Spain in great numbers—goldwork and jewellery, small glassware, decorated vases, small bronzes and religious statues—so that the Celtiberians became accustomed to the Graeco-Oriental aesthetic. And these products were toon imitated within the country. This was particularly the case for pottery, and above all for goldwork, a craft in which their own productions, the torcs we have described, show that they were already past masters. Henceforth the style from which they drew their inspiration was that of the Mediterranean world.

The first Greek and Phœnician trading posts

The first Phœnician settlements have been noted in Baetica, in south-west Spain, dating from the 11th century BC: the Tyrians founded a trading post at Gadir or Gades, the modern-day Cadiz. On the Mediterranean coast they held Abdera and Malaga.

In the 6th century before Christ the decline of the great commercial centre of Tyr in Phœnicia resulted in the transfer of their distant outposts into the hands of another Phœnician city: Carthage. Carthage had been founded by the Tyrians in the 9th century BC, and was at first only a staging-post for their fleet. But it declared independence in the 5th century BC and continued the commercial policy of Tyr to its own profit. It was subsequently obliged to confront that other colonising sea power, Greece.

It was the Phocaeans, coming from Asia Minor, who began a very early Greek colonisation in Spain. With this in mind they first set up an intermediate port of call, as had the Tyrians at Carthage: in this case it was Marseilles. The Greeks first took a foothold on the Spanish coast in the 8th century BC. There is, it is true, reference to the mythical Tartes-

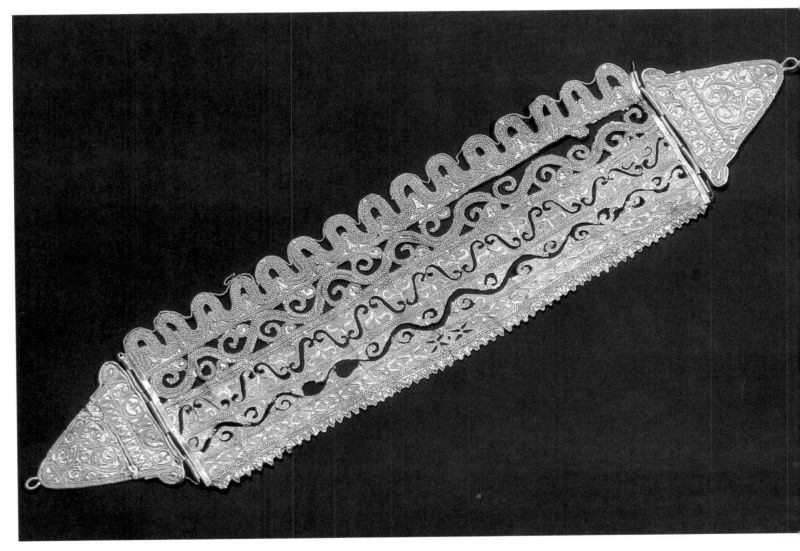

sos at the mouth of the Guadalquivir river, on the Atlantic, which was possibly established in the 9th century BC by the Phœnicians and is said to have later passed into the hands of the Greeks. But no excavation has so far confirmed the existence of this city, the name of which might also refer to the Iberian population of the south coast. The Greek colonies included above all Rhodae (Rosas), Emporion (Ampurias), Saguntum, Odysea and Mainake.

With the rise of the power of Carthage in the 5th and 4th centuries BC, the Greeks settled in Spain were forced towards the north-west. By the

Gold coronet in the Greek style with a filigree decoration, from the treasure of Javéa in Alicante province. It is a work of great delicacy dating from the sixth century BC (National Archaeological Museum, Madrid).

3rd century the Carthaginians had become masters of the western Mediterranean: they progressively seized all the islands, establishing bases on them for a war fleet that was to provide protection for the merchant ships: Majorca and Minorca, the Lipari and Aegates islands, Malta and Pantalleria, and of course Corsica, Sardinia and the western half of Sicily; all these belonged to Carthage. In addition they held almost all the north coast of Africa, from Tripolitania to Tangiers. They set up a series of trading posts such as Akra Leuka (Alicante), Ebussos (Ibiza) and above all the centre of their power in Spain, Mastia or Cartagena, a name which comes from the Carthaginian Qart Hasadat, "the new capital".

Eastern influences

The art, culture and religion of archaic and classical Greece which made a perceptible mark on Spain are well enough known. Less so is the character of the Phœnician and then Carthagian aesthetic. So it is worth our while to dwell a little on some aspects of this oriental art, a composite art which comes at the same time from the Egypt of the Pharaohs (which had for a long time held Phœnicia in its power) and from the influences of Syria and Mesopotamia. This double origin was already

A large bull's head in bronze, from a sanctuary to the Syro-Phœnician god Baal in Majorca. This god of fertility, represented here with a remarkable sobriety, could date from the fifth century BC (National Archaeological Museum, Madrid).

Right:
Terra cotta statuette known as the "Lady of Ibiza", representing the goddess Tanit, of Phœnician origin. It is a good example of the Carthaginian art of the sixth century BC, and shows this goddess of resurrection as she was seen before the arrival of the Greek influences one may see in the "Lady of Baza" or the "Lady of Elche". But like these other "ladies", she is already richly bejewelled.

visible between 2000 and 1000 BC in the artistic output of Byblos, one of the principal Phœnician ports along with Tyr and Sidon. It was to persist in Carthaginian art up to a relatively late date.

The range of artistic expression that reached the Spanish coast between 1000 BC and the birth of Christ thus summed up all the aesthetic forms represented from the coast of Anatolia to the Nile valley, through the Fertile Crescent. This multiplicity of currents working on Spain excluded any possibility of the birth of a homogenous style. Iberian Phœnician and Iberian Greek products reflect here one and here another of the arts of the eastern Mediterranean. A genuinely unified artistic expression was to emerge only with the period of Romanisation at the dawn of our own era. Rome alone was to impose a unification of Spain's artistic language.

The "Lady of Baza", from the province of Granada, was discovered in 1973 in a Carthaginian cemetery. This large statue, which must date from the fourth century BC, represents the goddess of death and resurrection, the Astarte of the Phœnicians, with the characteristics of the cosmic mother goddess, seated on an impressive throne and wearing rich gold decorations. A hollow in her back indicates that she was intended as a cinerary urn (National Archaeological Museum, Madrid).

The few examples we present here of Phœnician-Carthaginian works found on Spanish soil are revelatory: the little bronze statuette of a god with a golden mask, brought to light in Cadiz, has the classic pose of the god Ptah, worshipped by the Egyptians, while his gilded face is more evocative of the divinities of Byblos. The bulls' heads from Majorca, on the other hand, worked in bronze, are reminiscent of the Syro-Phœnician god Baal, symbol of fertility. And finally the "Lady of Galea" from Granada combines the winged sphinxes of Egypt and Babylon with the symbol of the great cosmic mothergod worshipped by all the peoples of the Near East. This figure is first among a whole series of "Ladies", as the Spanish have christened them. In fact in the "Lady of Ibiza" it is the image of Tanit-Astarte one sees, a goddess of resurrection. And even if this archaic terracotta figure, dating from the 7th century BC, is still a fairly crude work, sculptured figures of the same goddess made over the ensuing centuries were to be increasingly influenced by the Hellenic style.

This is so for example in the remarkable "Lady of Baza" unearthed in the province of Granada in 1973. This exceptional discovery showing the Mother goddess with the characteristics of Demeter, corresponding to Tanit-Astarte, has retained the rigorously full-face aspect of its prototypes. Seated on a solemn throne she is wearing a full robe, soberly draped, and she is richly bejewelled. It is a recent find, shedding some light on the most famous of the Spanish female divinities, the "Lady of Elche". This masterpiece of the Iberian heritage, discovered in 1897, had remained a mystery as regards its purpose. But the Lady of Elche, like the Lady of Baza, has a cavity in her back; and the Lady of Baza was brought to light in a necropolis, where she stood with her back against

The famous "Lady of Elche", masterpiece of Iberic art, representing the Phœnician goddess Astarte-Demeter. This sculpture in stone, from the fifth or fourth century BC, shows the high degree of development in Spanish art on the eve of the Roman intervention (National Archaeological Museum, Madrid).

Right:
The Lion of Baena, near Cordova, is a good example of the Iberians' stylised representation of animals (National Archaeological Museum, Madrid).

Silver patera from the treasure of San-tisteban de Puerto, in the Jaen region: Classical silversmith's work which may go back to the third century BC and represents a crown of centaurs capering around a lion's head in high relief (National Archaeological Museum, Madrid).

one wall of a tomb, funerary ashes still in her cavity. So she was in fact a cinerary urn bearing the face of the goddess of death and resurrection.

This famous "Lady of Elche" from Alicante province, her perfect, severe and haughty face bearing a strong imprint of Greek influences, wears a rich ornamentation of gold: a coronet, two rich and curious tambourine-shaped objects in highly-worked filigree which frame her face and are probably combs to keep her hair in place, a triple row of necklaces from which hang little amphorae symbolising lustral water, and heavy pendant ear-rings. As with the "Lady of Baza", remnants of polychrome suggest that the work was originally highly coloured in the manner of the Hellenic "kores".

Particular archaeological discoveries allow us to imagine the delicacy and virtuosity of the gold jewellery that is imitated on these statuettes.

Preceding page :
A beautiful bronze head which probably represents the emperor Augustus (first century BC). Found at Azaila in the province of Teruel, it counts among the best examples of Classical Roman portrait art (National Archaeological Museum, Madrid).

The gold coronet from the Javea treasure, in Alicante province, for example : this shows a quite exceptional mastery of filigree, treated in a style bearing a strong Greek influence. Or again the silver patera from the Santisteban de Puerto hoard, from Jaen province, with its decoration of centaurs around a lion's head in high relief, this too in a very Greek style.

The penetration of Rome

Founded in 814 BC, Carthage grew steadily in importance and became, during the third century BC at the time of the Punic Wars, the main adversary of a rising Roman power. The Punic Wars were to end only with the destruction of Carthage in 146 BC. Rome in the meantime had become a maritime power and was now able to reign supreme over the Mediterranean Basin.

Although there had long since been Phœnician bases in Spain, the Carthagian occupation of the peninsula, properly speaking, dates only from 237 BC : the forces of the Barca clan, at the end of the first Punic

The remains of the Roman tomb at Servilia, near Carmona in the Seville region, constitute a veritable necropolis which is partly cut out of the rock and partly built up : the hypogea stand next to sanctuaries dedicated to the cult of the dead.

Right :
Cut into the tuff-stone, the domed hall in the tomb at Servilia, with its oculus and the curious groins carved in imitation of the structure of Roman building methods.

war, decided to establish themselves here, create a prosperous colony and exploit the Spanish mines. Hasdrubal, the father of Hannibal, founded the city of Cartagena in 228, as the new capital of the Punic territories, preferring this to Carthage itself, which was too close to Italy for safety.

Rome undestood very well the threat posed by such a dynamic Carthaginian empire in Spain, and only awaited the right pretext to intervene. In 219 BC Rome accused Hannibal of having overstepped the limits defined in an earlier treaty between the two powers by seizing Saguntum, even though this city seems in fact to have been well within Carthaginian territory, lying as it does to the south of the river Ebre, demarcation line between the two powers. This was the dispute that launched the second Punic war. The Romans disembarked at Emporium in 218, but were unable to maintain their position in the face of 60,000 men at arms drawn up by Hannibal to carry the war overland onto Roman soil, crossing the Perthus, southern Gaul and the Alps. After almost defeating Rome through a whole series of striking victories on the Tessin and Trebia rivers, at Trasimenus and at Cannes, Hannibal was finally defeated in 202, on the mainland of Africa, at Zama, where Scipio had disembarked.

Overleaf (pages 24-25):
Frons scenae of the Roman theatre at Merida, built in AD 18, but enriched with two tiers of colonnades in the second century. It constitutes one of the most perfect examples of Roman secular architecture in the imperial age. The remarkable restoration that has been carried out on it shows to good advantage the "baroque" spirit of this symbolic facade with its projections and recesses.

The ruins of the amphitheatre at Italica, home of the emperors Trajan and Hadrian in the AD second century. 156 metres long by 134 wide (170 yards by 146) the amphitheatre could accommodate nearly 30,000 spectators. In the centre, the cellars where the wild beasts were kept before they entered the ring.

Rome took advantage of this victory to annexe Spain. But the occupation of the country met with fierce resistance from the Celtiberians, who rose in revolt in 181, in 154 and again in 144 BC. This last rebellion, led in Lusitania by the Hispanic war lord Viriatus, was marked by the tragic end of Numantia, near Soria, a fortified city which Scipio Aemilianus finally seized at the end of an eight-year siege and a blockade lasting fifteen months, an operation that required 60,000 men—a force as large as that rallied by the Carthaginians to launch their attack on the Roman republic! The heroic Celtiberian defenders refused to surrender, preferring suicide to capture by the Roman enemy. The town was razed to the ground, and its end was the end too of the long period of resistance to Rome's presence in Spain.

The provinces of Hither Spain, later the region of Tarraconensis, and Farther Spain, later divided into Lusitania and Baetica, were connected to the Italian mainland by the annexation of Transalpine Gaul and the Narbonne region, and the foundation of colonies at Aix and Narbonne in 122 and 118 respectively. From this point on Rome's efforts went into merging together all the coastal lands around the Mediterranean into one vast entity, the "Imperial Republic" around the "Mare Nostrum" of the Mediterranean. Spain was to play an appreciable rôle within this perspective, starting with the establishment of an active policy of

Found in Cordova in 1958, this great marble sarcophagus dates from the AD third century and shows the dead being led, each one by his own guide, to the gates of Hades. The barley-sugar twisted columns and the rich architecture of the doorway with its pediment show the art of the empire in its fullest maturity (Alcazar Museum, Cordova).

View along the Roman aqueduct at Segovia. Its 128 arches in two tiers, built in granite blocks, span a depression some 30 metres (100 feet) deep. It is one of the best examples of Roman hydraulic engineering.

Facing page, left:
The old Roman bridge across the Guadalquivir river at Cordova, 240 metres (260 yards) long, dates back to the days of Augustus but has been several times restored. In the background, the silhouette of the cathedral standing within the Umayyad mosque.

Facing page, top left:
Roman bronze statuette representing an athlete, from Pallensa in Majorca. Inspired by the art of Classical Greece, this little bronze has been worked with great mastership (National Archaeological Museum, Madrid).

Facing page, bottom:
Still functioning today, the Roman baths at Alange near Merida, with the dome 11 metres (36 feet) in diameter and light provided by an oculus, where one may still take a water cure in the marble pool.

urbanisation aimed at uniting the indigenous peoples and the Roman colonists.

This urbanisation was carried out by the building of cities that were purely Roman in character. They were based on a road communication system and on the adoption of unified and unifying architectural formulae responding to the needs of a centralised system of government, a centralised religion, and a centralised military regime. These Roman towns were all alike in their regular Hippodamian-style town plan, originating in Roman military camps and also used for garrisons, and in their urban framework of public buildings providing a whole programme to meet the empire's social, religious and political needs. The same religious system, the same municipal administrative buildings and identical public leisure facilities were brought to the far ends of the territories occupied by that "universal power" that Rome aspired to be. Temples, fora, markets, theatres and amphitheatres, baths: these were the constituent parts of the imperial architecture imposed on the provinces. A water supply system based on aqueducts—all the more important in Spain where the lands of the Meseta receive little rainfall—completed the typical infrastructure of Roman town planning. Around this monumental framework grew the city and its houses with their atria, mosaics, porticos, statuary and painted decoration.

Romanisation made its most spectacular progress, and the country saw its greatest period of glory, in the time of Augustus and then under the reigns of Trajan and Hadrian—both of whom, it should not be forgotten, were of Spanish origin. During this period the Latin language, the culture and arts and way of life of the Romans spread across the country from the coastal areas inland, as had all earlier influences with the one exception of the Celtic. This "cultural colonisation" progressed at the price of the extinction of an indigenous culture which had been, on the eve of integration into the empire, in its full flower of expansion, as the "Lady of Baza" and the "Lady of Elche" demonstrate. For the unified culture imposed by Rome and in which the Iberian peninsula henceforth took part was intolerant of local particularities. Indigenous trends were forced to make way for the grand imperial style in sculpture, painting and architecture from the Atlantic to the frontiers of Persia and from Britain to the Sahara.

Archaeological wealth

The traveller through Spain in often astonished to find Roman remains as imposing and well-preserved as, for example, the ruins of the once-great city of Merida—Augusta Emerita of Roman times, capital of Lusitania and founded in 25 BC. Here can be seen a remarkable Roman theatre, which has had the colonnades along the back wall of the stage

re-erected; it counts among the best preserved "frons scenae" in the empire, along with those in the theatres at Lepcis Magna and Sabratha in Libya. With seating for 6,000 spectators, it is a good indication of the wealth of this city built along the "silver route" that led from the Cantabrian mines. The remains of the amphitheatre, built to accommodate 16,000, are however overshadowed by the arenas at Italica, a colony founded by Scipio the African in 206 BC; these arenas were built by Trajan for 25,000 to 30,000 enthusiasts of the Romans' ferocious bloodsports. Near Merida, there is also the almost incredible surprise of a Roman bath complex still in use today: Alange has in fact two domed halls more than 11 metres (36 feet) in diameter and lit by means of oculi, as in the Pantheon at Rome.

Or again, it is equally astonishing to learn that the great aqueduct at Segovia, 813 metres (890 yards) long and with 128 arches, overlooking the town from some 30 metres (100 feet) up, is still in use, and supports a water course supplying the conurbation. And the great aqueduct at Tarragona, near the former town of Tarraco, comparable to the famous Pont du Gard, still stands intact in the countryside. Finally the Roman bridges at Cordova, Merida, Salamanca and Alcantara bear witness to the genius of the Roman engineers; today they carry unyieldingly the weight of trucks and heavyweight lorries.

Nowhere is it a question of a provincial, secondary art: for Spain took its full part in Roman culture. Seneca was born in Cordova, Quintilian, Lucanus and Martial also came from Spain: the world of literature as well as the fine arts shone brilliantly in this Iberian land which also gave Rome two of its most glorious emperors—Trajan and Hadrian.

Visigoth Kings and Arab Invasion

Visigothic capital from the church of San Pedro de la Nave, representing Daniel in the lions' den. Daniel has prostrated himself in prayer between the two lions, a gesture which has survived, in this bible illustration, from early Christianity.

Another capital that tells a story in the church of San Pedro de la Nave, built around AD 680: Abraham's sacrifice told in carving. Abraham has placed a faggot on the altar and is about to sacrifice his son, but the hand of God appears to the left, and the ram is caught in the bush. The sculptor may have drawn inspiration from a Visigothic miniature.

The Iberian peninsula became Christian early on: already in the third century Tertullian tells us that there are Christians throughout the country. But from time to time imperial persecutions forced them to seek refuge in the hinterland.

The precepts of the new Church were not, however, unified: heretic voices were raised within the Christian community, such as that of Arius, a priest from Alexandria who in AD 320 denied the divinity of Christ and defied his bishop. His thesis was that Christ was only the Father's "minister", a mediator who himself worshipped God the Father.

As early as 325, with Arianism spreading across the empire, a Spanish priest by the name of Osius, born in Cordova, called on Constantine to convene a religious council. This was Nicaea, the Church's first "œ-

cumenical" council. Osius drew up the Nicene Creed and condemned Arianism. The zeal of this prelate is to be explained by the progress the heresy had made in Spain. In 381, Theodosius confirmed the Nicene council's condemnation and passed a law against the Arian sect.

The end of the Antiquity

Historians are generally in agreement in dating the end of the Universal Roman Empire to the emperor Theodosius' decision to divide the Roman world in two: the Western Empire and the Eastern Empire.

When Theodosius died in 395 he decided that his son Arcadius should rule over the East while his other heir, Honorius, should take the West. The same year, under the leadership of Alaric, the Visigoths, until then federated in the empire, revolted; they set siege first to Constantinople and then to Athens; Stilicon the Vandal stopped their advance with the troops he commanded as defender of the empire. But on December 31st 406, there was a reverse stampede: Vandals, Sarmatians, Alans, Suevians and Alamanni, pushed on by the Huns, crossed the Rhine. The Vandals and Suevians pushed forward their offensive, crossed Gaul and invaded Spain in 409. The Alans rejoined them and reached the rivers Tajo and Duero; Vandals and Suevians settled in Galicia and Asturia. In 410, Alaric seized Rome and put it to plunder. A few months later he died, and was succeeded by Ataulf who, with his Visigoths, took control of southern Gaul. In AD 414 he married Galla Placidia, captive daughter of the emperor Theodosius. Even so the government at Ravenna declared war on him; so Ataulf crossed the Pyrenees and occupied Tarraconensis. The whole of Spain had become a battlefield on which the Barbarians fought it out among themselves. The Vandals established themselves in Andalusia in 423, then in 429 moved on into Africa with Genseric at their head. In 438 the Suevians, having left Galicia, held the whole of southern Spain.

The Visigothic church of San Pedro de la Nave near Zamora, dating from about 680. The lantern over the crossing has been restored; the tall transept is prolonged by two projecting porches. The square choir is lit only by tiny windows.

The Visigothic kingdom

Faced with the invasion of Attila and the Huns, the Franks and the Visigoths under Theodoric's leadership allied with Aetius' imperial troops and in 451 forced the Huns back into the Catalaunian Fields. But Theodoric fell at the head of his troops. His son Euric occupied the whole of Spain. And though even the fiction of a Roman empire was dead by 476, the Visigothic king was to set up his own authority to fill the power vacuum; Euric copied the protocol of the Roman empire and created a Visigothic code of law. But he was an Arian; for although outlawed within the empire, Arianism had flourished among the Christianised Barbarians—they had taken up Arius' cause even before its condemnation at Nicaea. And it was among the Visigoths of Spain that the heresy became most firmly established. The Arian monarchy of the Visigothic kings of Toledo opposed the Catholicism of the great majority of the Spanish population: Arianism became the state religion.

A Visigothic belt clasp discovered at Carpio del Tajo in the province of Toledo. The bronze plaque is ornamented with cut garnets and blue semi-precious stones treated in cloisonné style (National Archaelogical Museum, Madrid).

Right:
Two fine fibulas in the form of eagles, from Catalayud and probably dating from the sixth century AD. The set garnets and heraldic forms are quite distinct from Classical forms: this is the "barbarian" art of a nomadic people (National Archaeological Museum, Madrid).

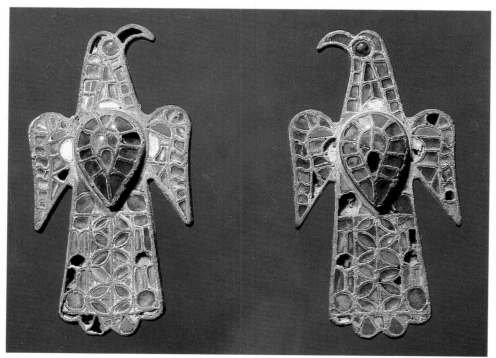

Toledo was now the Visigoth capital, and the bishop of Toledo primate of Spain. He ruled a Church in which the service was in the Gothic language. The calendar too was quite particular, for it set the start of our era thirty-eight years earlier than the rest of the Christian world, a computation that remained in force until the 11th century.

The Arian Visigothic kings were frequently at war with the Franks, who laid waste the region of Tarragona. Quarrels over the succession and the Black Death that decimated Spain in 543 made their mark on these confused times. The Eastern Empire regained its strength and Justinian, hoping to win back for Byzantium the former Roman possessions in the West, reconquered the south and east of Spain in 554. This reconquest was of short duration, however, and within twenty years the western lands had begun to escape from Byzantine control.

When Leovgild acceded to power in Toledo in 573, the country became progressively reunified in both ethnic and religious terms. By marrying a Catholic, Theodosia, sister of the bishops of Seville Leander and Isidore, Leovgild effectively hastened the fusion of Visigoths and Hispano-Romans. He also supported Catholic ideas on the divine nature of Christ, the main point of divergence between the Arians and the religious orthodoxy. This essential concession robbed Arianism of its substance. And to make peace with the Franks he had his son Hermenegild marry the Catholic great-granddaughter of Clovis.

With the support of the Byzantine emperor Maurice, Hermenegild

Masterpiece of the treasure of Guarrazar near Toledo, the votive crown of king Recceswinth was discovered in 1859. It must have hung over the altar in the royal chapel at Toledo. This superb piece of Visigothic goldsmith's craft, dating from 650-672, is a quite exceptional work with its polished stones set in the pierced gold of the crown and enriched by a series of pendents which make up the words "Recesvinthus Rex" (National Archaeological Museum Madrid).

rose in revolt in 583 and was then converted to Catholicism. But he was killed, and was succeeded by his brother Reccared. Reccared too embraced the Catholic faith; at the Council of Toledo in 589 he solemnly renounced Arianism, followed by the court and the heretic bishops. All recited the Nicene Creed. Arianism was never more to be the official religion of the Gothic state, but its effects lingered on.

The conversion of Reccared led the Byzantines to make peace with the Visigoths. But war broke out anew, and Svintila (621-631) twice inflicted defeat on the Byzantines, driving them out of their last territories on the Spanish coast.

The Isidorian revival

By the end of Arianism in the Visigothic monarchy, certain social circles were turning anew to the great Roman tradition of erudition and culture. Thus Seville, where the brothers Leander (579-600) and Isidore (600-636) were bishops, became once again a brilliant seat of learning. Indeed Isidore of Seville is the greatest figure of the Spanish church in the days of the Visigoths. He was, in addition, the most illustrious teacher of the Middle Ages. He wrote the "Etymologies", a work in twenty volumes which represented the sum of the knowledge of his day. It is a huge compilation of Greek and Roman treatises on geometry, astronomy, architecture, the naval arts, grammar, metaphysics, literature, theology and liturgy. Through his influence the Latin language regained its prestige. In addition, in his "History of the Goths" he developed a Spanish "nationalism" of his own.

Visigothic belt buckle in bronze, decorated with reliefs showing two lions face to face: this is the old Mesopotamian theme of the lions of Gilgamesh on either side of a Tree of Life which has been introduced by the nomadic Visigoths. The clasp could date from the sixth century (National Archaeological Museum, Madrid).

This Isidorian revival fell at the same time as the royal court's return to Catholicism. And succeeding the Arian dignitaries, the new archbishop of Toledo became in his turn primate of all Spain. The religious rite was henceforth unified throughout the country. No Barbarian state had ever given so dominant a place to the Church; the king became involved in the affairs of the Church and nominated the bishops, and the high clergy were involved in decisions of state to such an extent that their councils functioned almost as a parliament. The king tolerated no non-Catholic within the kingdom, and there was considerable persecution of the Jews. The clergy constrained the king to elaborate a law common to Visigoths and Hispano-Romans alike, through which the fusion of the two national communities was achieved.

Further strengthened by the Councils of Toledo, the privileges of the clergy became exorbitant. King Chindaswinth sought to combat this tendency and brought his son Recceswinth onto the throne with him. Recceswinth was to create the "Liber Judiciorum", a law designed on the model of the Code of Justinian, and enacted in 654.

Visigothic art

Fruit of a migratory population emerging from eastern Europe and the plains of Russia, Visigothic art included at first only easily-transported items: jewellery, belt-clasps, fibulas, bridle and harness decorations. This "barbarian" art, worked in gold or bronze enhanced by large cut garnets or pearls and rock crystal, is in a formal artistic language that rejects entirely the tradition of Roman art. It is a considerable rupture; the mode of expression has nothing in common with that of the classical repertoire.

Further, the specifically Spanish tendencies which had been so long stifled during the period of Roman rule were able to re-emerge after the invasions, with their decorative motifs originating in pre-history—solar wheels and stylised animals.

In the field of architecture, it is first and foremost to be deplored that so few Visigothic works have survived to our day. The destruction that followed on the Arab invasion and the wars of the Reconquista, then the elimination of churches become too small for the population in the Middle Ages, the Renaissance and again in the Baroque period, have deprived us of a quantity of creations which would have been of great

The square chevet of the Visigothic church of Quintanilla de las Viñas in Burgos province, built around AD 700. Note the bands of decoration that separate the courses of large dressed stone, a frieze of interlacing vines forming circles within which mingle geometric and floral motifs in bas-relief.

33

value in giving us a clear idea of this art born at the turning-point between lower Antiquity and the high Middle Ages.

In particular, the court architecture of Toledo has entirely disappeared, but for a few relief carvings on pillars and lintels. In addition the only significant testimony we do have dates from the last period, that of the Isidorian revival, after the conversion of the Arian Visigoths to Catholicism. In fact the main architectural works we know date from the second half of the 7th century. We know nothing at all of the sanctuaries and palaces of the Visigothic kingdom in its Arian period. And finally, specialists have not always been in agreement on the age of such sadly rare buildings as do survive, for a frequent use of re-cycled building materials makes dating difficult.

What first strikes the visitor who stands before these buildings is their relatively small size. Most of the churches, in any other age, would be regarded as chapels. This modesty of size is as much the result of the general poverty of the time and of the decrease in the population following the great invasions as of any absence of the technology necessary to build vast internal spaces. It may be that larger buildings existed in such urban centres as Toledo, Cordova, Merida or Seville, but archaeologists have not found their traces.

The Visigothic church of San Juan de Baños, near Palencia, bears the date of 661 and was therefore built under the reign of king Recceswinth. The structure above the door is a later addition.

Facing page:
The nave and choir of the Visigothic church of San Juan de Baños: the body of the church is divided into three aisles by arcades whose columns are recycled Roman works and whose archaic capitals derive from the acanthus carvings of Antique capitals. The square chevet has a horseshoe vault, and the arches in the nave too are horseshoe arches.

The surviving monuments

The finest of the Visigothic churches, San Pedro de la Nave, is one example of the arguments over dating that we have mentioned. At first considered to be a 9th century work, it is today dated to the second half of the 7th century. As one comes across the deeply undulating country of the Campo de Zamora between Salamanca and Leon, the little village of El Campillo, crowned by the church of San Pedro de la Nave, appears in a fold between hills: nothing suggests that here is one of the most remarkable reconstructions of medieval archaeology. It all seems to have remained untouched for centuries, so successfully has it been integrated into its site. But in fact in 1930, before the construction of the dam which would have drowned it, the church was entirely dismantled to be reconstructed beyond reach of the waters.

What is striking in this building with its harmonious proportions and carefully-scaled, studied volume, is the readability of its plan, based on an inscribed Greek cross of Byzantine origin. The total length does not exceed 23 metres (75 feet); the nave, flanked by side aisles, leads to a crossing with lateral porches that prolong the transept. A square apse completes the building beyond a choir flanked by sacristies. All is built in fine, regular dressed stone, evocative both of Roman Africa and of the churches of Syria.

Besides the discreet decoration of vines and wheel-forms around the body of the church, we would emphasise the fine capitals that top the columns of the crossing. The two most important represent Daniel in the lions' den and Abraham about to sacrifice his son. Their style remains close to some palaeochristian art, particularly in Daniel's gesture of prayer.

San Juan of Baños is one Visigothic church with the advantage of an exact dating: an inscription engraved in the marble corresponds to 661. The nave includes recycled antique columns, their capitals copied from Roman works, but with their acanthus leaves treated in a simplified style which is purely Visigothic. These support a series of horseshoe arches; and here we should mention that the horseshoe arch was not originally an Islamic invention as was thought for so long, but dates back to the end of the imperial Roman age, as witness many Roman-Iberian funerary steles in Spain which combine such arches with pre-historic solar wheels.

As to Quintanilla de la Viñas in the Burgos region, it is built like the above two churches in regular dressed stone, but on the outside also has a rich decoration in bands all round the choir. The motifs of these bas-

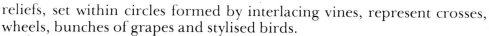

Lying along the banks of the Guadiana river, the fortified wall of the Alcazaba of Abd er-Rahman II was built in 835 in Merida for the town's Arab garrison. But the Moslem architects have used the Roman foundations of a previous wall to a height of 7 metres (23 feet) throughout its length.

reliefs, set within circles formed by interlacing vines, represent crosses, wheels, bunches of grapes and stylised birds.

An examination of these sadly rare relics of their time shows a varied architectural language, often with a Byzantine influence, but characterised by their modest dimensions. In the royal city of Toledo it seems unlikely that the court would content itself with such rustic chapels—such buildings could not measure up to the glorious "Order of the Goths" to which the texts refer.

Only the smaller articles that have survived can give us an idea of this splendour, for example the remarkable discovery of 1859, the treasure from Guarrazar near Toledo. It is made up essentially of votive crowns. These would have hung in the choir of the royal church, following a Byzantine tradition going back to Justinian's day; their purpose was to bring down the blessings of god onto the sovereign. One of these crowns, made of perforated gold sections offset by pearls, mounted polished stones and cloisonnés with or without coloured enamels, has long dangling pendants in the form of letters spelling out "Recesvinthus Rex", and can thus be accurately dated to the reign of this Visigoth king between 649 and 672.

The little mosque of Bab al-Mardom in Toledo, known now as the church of Santo Cristo de la Luz (Christ of Light), was built in 980. The front decoration of intersecting arches is typical of the art of the caliphate.

Right:
Interior of the Aljaferia in Saragossa, a fortified Arab palace which was the residence of the emirs of Aragon from the ninth to the eleventh centuries. This part of the building was constructed in about 1050: interlaced multifoil arches and light colonnettes which are recycled Visigothic works.

The end of the Visigoths

Vamba, successor to Recceswinth, turned Toledo into a city of great luxury. The court was at the summit of its glory; nowhere in Europe was there a comparable renaissance of civilisation. But this brilliant period ended in anarchy—coups d'Etat and palace conspiracies followed one on another. Ervigius, a Byzantine who had usurped the throne of Toledo, authorised a tax cut, abolished penalties against those who failed to fulfil their military obligations, and reduced the army.

The country slid into chaos: famine, a fresh epidemic of plague and incursions by the Franks accelerated the decline; then the country was torn by civil war between the partisans of Roderick and those of Akhila. The latter took refuge in Ceuta, where the town governor advised him to call on the Arabs for help against Roderick. Such was the origin of the Islamic invasion, to which the world of the Visigoths was to succumb within less than ten years.

For rather less than a hundred years, the Arab nation had been on the march, motivated by the new faith preached by the Prophet Mohammed

Carved ivory box made in 964 for a favourite of the caliph al-Hakam of Cordova, and found in Zamora. Two peacocks face each other amid deeply-carved foliage (National Archaeological Museum, Madrid).

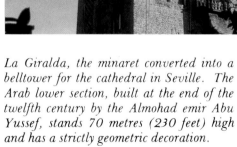

La Giralda, the minaret converted into a belltower for the cathedral in Seville. The Arab lower section, built at the end of the twelfth century by the Almohad emir Abu Yussef, stands 70 metres (230 feet) high and has a strictly geometric decoration.

Top right:
The Aljibe or Arab reservoir from Cáceres, built in 1151 by Alha el-Gami on the model of the Byzantine reservoirs with columns.

Ivory casket made of carved ivory plaques by eleventh-century Arab craftsmen, and made up as a reliquary with enamelled metal mountings during the Romanesque age. It was part of the treasure of San Isidore de Leon (National Archaeological Museum, Madrid).

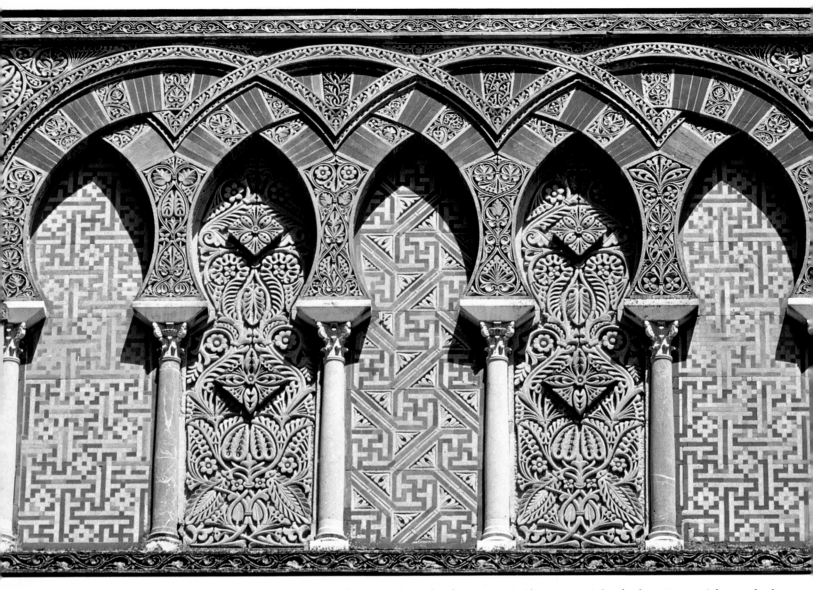

Detail of the decoration on the west front of the Great Mosque at Cordova. This part, built at the time of the enlargements under al-Hakam II around AD 961, shows the richness of Islamic ornament, with its interlaced arches with alternating elements of stone, brick and stucco. Geometric motifs and carved vines alternate in a skilful combination.

in Arabia. They had successively vanquished the Sassanids and the Byzantines, and by the dawn of the eighth century had reached simultaneously Chinese Turkestan and the Atlantic.

The Islamic forces, led by the Berber Tarik, disembarked near Gibraltar (Gebel el-Tarik, the Mountain of Tarik) in 711—a fateful day in the history of Spain. Tarik defeated Roderick, the last king of the Visigoths, in a battle beside the river Guadelate. The king was killed in the battle, his troops crushed. The knights of Islam seized Cordova, rode on to Toledo which surrendered, then rode north to seize Astorga, capital of Asturia, and finally Lugo in Galicia, before turning south again to Segovia in 712. The conquest of Spain was carried out like a simple military march.

In 714, Spain recognised and accepted Moslem domination. The country was now called al-Andalus, a name which has remained attached to the southern part of the country, the region in which this "colonisation" lasted longest.

The weakness of the Visigothic kingdom's resistance, undermined as it was by internal quarrels, and its sudden collapse, robbed the Christians of all their hopes. Henceforth they were once again forced into the background as the Catholics had been in the days of Arianism. And the domination of Islam was to last nearly eight hundred years on Spanish soil.

Tarik's Berber troops amounted to only seven thousand men; Musa's Arab army cannot have been much larger. When the Moslems decided to establish their capital at Cordova, where there remained a lively Roman substratum, it was not from this unpolished Arab and Berber soldiery that a refined civilisation could grow and flourish. But they were soon followed by several tens of thousands of men from the east, and it was in particular the Mozarabs, the Christians who lived within Arab society, who contributed to a revival. Many of these even converted to Islam to escape the taxes imposed on non-Moslems.

It was thus first of all the Visigothic heritage which was drawn upon, alongside the Arab literature, architecture and arts from the already highly sophisticated Umayyad world of Damascus and Jerusalem. What resulted was an original and powerful Hispano-Moorish art, to which Byzantine modes of expression contributed, as in the Near East, a considerable enrichment.

In addition, the dramatic end of the Umayyad dynasty in Damascus in 750 and the flight of the sole survivor of the massacred family to Spain earned the Arab culture its vigorous expansion in this Far West of the Islamic world. This refugee, Abd er-Rahman, who proclaimed himself Emir of al-Andalus after defeating the established governor in battle, was heir to the high administrative organisation and the impressive civilisation that had developed in Damascus. By 788, he controlled the whole of Moslem Spain and sought to create here a reflection of his lost homeland. Two years earlier he had founded the Great Mosque at Cordova, which was to be unceasingly enlarged over the next two centuries.

Overleaf (pages 40-41):
The great hypostyle hall of the Mosque at Cordova, founded in 786, then enlarged in 822, 961 and 988. In its final state it included nearly six hundred columns supporting a double arcade. The arches, in alternating arch-stones of brick and stone, are semi-circular in the upper range and horseshoed below. The ceiling is in raftered timber.

The octagonal cupola with intersecting arches, forming two squares at an angle of 45° to each other, over the mihrab of the Great Mosque in Cordova. Built in the time of al-Hakam II in the tenth century, the dome has a mosaic decoration worked by Byzantine artists. Note the octagon around the central dome, with an inscription in kufic characters around it.

Arab, Asturian and Mozarab Art

The chevet of the Asturian church of Santullano (San Julian de los Prados) in Oviedo, built in the early ninth century by Alfonso the Chaste.

The presence of the Arabs in Spain resulted from the eighth century on in the production of works of art of prime importance. But it was not until the early ninth century that artistic activity on the Christian side, interrupted by the collapse of the Visigoths, revived.

Islamic works

We do not here have space to outline the evolution of Islamic architecture in Spain: fortifications and castles, mosques and palaces. We will restrict ourselves to a description of one monument which sums up the essential characteristics of this art, and which took it to its zenith: the Great Mosque at Cordova, built by the Umayyads and begun in 786.

Built in Cordova, capital of the emirate and later, from 929, capital of the Umayyad caliphate of Spain, this mosque is made up of an immense hypostyle with a courtyard in front and, above it, a tall quadrangular minaret. The prayer hall is the outcome of numerous enlargements carried out in 822, 912, 961 and 988. In its final state—before the further transformations carried out after the Christian Reconquista—the building counted some six hundred columns, many of them recycled elements from Hispano-Roman buildings and demolished Visigothic churches. The mosque was thus the biggest hall ever built by the Moslems in the Mediterranean basin. This fact alone is proof of the size of the population converted to Islam in the Spanish capital.

The prayer hall of the mosque at Cordova in fact totals 130 metres by 110 (142 yards by 120) a covered area of over 1.5 hectare (3 acres). The structure supporting its flat wooden roof is composed of double arcades—probably inspired by the Roman aqueduct at Merida—in eighteen rows of columns at right angles to the qibla, the wall towards which the faithful turn to pray. The building thus presents a subtle play between the semi-circular arches of the upper level and the horseshoe arches of the lower arcade. The columns' marble shafts form a veritable forest, stretching as far as the eye can see.

As far as the structure of the building is concerned, the most interesting element is the ribbed cupola, dating from 961, over the mihrab. The mihrab of a mosque is normally a niche to indicate the direction for prayer, but in this instance it takes the form of a fully hexagonal chamber. The cupola over this holy of holies has eight equal intersecting arches supported by slender colonnettes. The mosaic decoration that covers this whole structure together with the frame around the mihrab's entrance has a gold ground upon which vines, branches and verses from the Koran in kufic script unfold. It was Byzan-

tine artists who carried out the work. Around the mihrab's entrance is a further framework of elaborate marble facings, deeply carved with floral decorations.

All this Cordovan Islamic art is of a highly refined character. It is court architecture endowed with a haughty grandeur, expressing the perfection and rigour of a technical skill at the pinnacle of its development. Through it the caliphate has left the mark of its power and wealth.

This richness can be seen again at Medina az-Zahara, a few miles outside Cordova, where the caliph Abd er-Rahman III had an immense palace built in 936. It is a veritable palatine and administrative city, covering over two hundred acres. The whole complex spreads out on terraces cut into the hillside with gardens, pools, reception halls, administrative buildings, barracks, a mosque and the royal residence itself. Comparable in style to the Great Mosque, this superb complex was pillaged and plundered in 1010, when the caliph's dynasty fell.

Finally the minor arts too shone with remarkable brilliance during

The Cross of the Angels from the treasure of Oviedo: ordered by Alfonso II, king of Asturia, and made in 808, this gold votive cross decorated with delicate filigree, polished stones and Romanesque intaglio work, measures no less than 46 centimetres (17½ inches) across. With its circular centre and arms that widen at the ends, this work became the symbol of the Asturian kingdom, for it represented the legendary cross of light that appeared to Pelayo at the battle of Covadonga.

this period: brocades and damask, carved ivories, bronzes, decorated weaponry and glazed ceramics.

The Asturian kingdom

But to see how a Christian resistance to the Islamic occupation came to be organised in the north of the peninsula, let us return to the days just after the Islamic invasion. As the Arab army advanced towards Narbonne and into Frankish territory, a very localised uprising broke out in the extreme north of Spain, in the mountainous region of Asturia. In these high valleys overshadowed by the Picos de Europa, Roman and Visigothic influence had always remained marginal, and now the Moslem authorities had the same difficulty in imposing their control.

It was among these fierce mountain dwellers, in a countryside that lent itself to such a revolt against the occupying forces, that a few Visigoth resistants sought refuge from the Moslem repression, coming from Toledo and the south. They settled in this forgotten region to await their moment for an uprising.

And here it was that Pelayo, heir to the last Visigoth king, fleeing Cordova, organised the rebellion. The Asturians listened to Pelayo, called

In the Asturian mountains, the little church of Santa Cristina de Lena, dating from 852, stands on an isolated outcrop at Vega del Rey in Oviedo province. It is symmetrical along both axes and has external buttressing.

an assembly and elected him their chief—following the tradition of the Visigoths, whose sovereigns had always been elected. In 718 the rebels decided to withdraw from the payment of tributes, and to attack the small Berber garrisons that controlled the region. The Arabs did not at first react to the rebellion; then in 722 they sent a punitive expedition under the Berber commander Alqama. Pelayo withdrew with his troops into the gorges of Covadonga, where he drew the Moslems into an ambush. Alqama fell in the battle and his troops were cut to pieces.

Their leader lost, the vanquished Moslem forces fled through the mountains, harassed as they went by the Asturian partisans. After two days and nights they reached Cosgaya on the steep banks of the river Deva; and here a landslide wiped out the survivors of the rout at

The Asturian palace of Naranco, near
Oviedo, built in 842 by the king Ramiro I,
is known today as the church of Santa
María de Naranco. The solidity of its rec-
tangular mass is lightened by the elegant
columned galleries.

Bottom:
The little church of San Salvador de
Valdedios, dating from the reign of Alfonso
the Great, was consecrated in 893 and
marks the last phase of Asturian architecture.

Asturian bas-relief decorating a door jamb
at the entrance to the church of San Miguel
de Lillo in Naranco. The theme of juggler
and lion-tamer reproduces that of a sixth-
century ivory consular diptych, though the
classicism of the diptych is here transformed
into expressionism.

Covadonga. Soon to be regarded as a miracle and attributed to the
Virgin, the landslide was interpreted as a providential sign. Pelayo, as
first king of Asturia, thus became the natural leader of the Christians
against the invaders, and established his capital at Cangas de Onis.

Before long, the Mozarabs—those Christians who lived among the
Moslems without renouncing their own faith—began to trickle north
towards freedom. They swelled the ranks of the independent Christians
and at the same time brought with them the echoes of the high Islamic
culture of Cordova. They thus contributed to an ecclesiastic restoration,
a renaissance of Christian civilisation, and began to build new
monasteries—an activity forbidden them in Islamic territory. It was
these refugees who implanted Mozarab art forms in the north of Spain.

In 739, Alfonso I came to the throne and gave a broader geographical
base to the little Asturian kingdom by seizing Galicia. In 749 he retook
Astorga and, in order to provide a protective barrier to the south, he
initiated a scorched earth policy and "turned the Gothic Fields into

desert as far as the Duero". In 775 Silo, king of Asturia, moved his capital to Pravia. In 788 Bermudo I once again shifted the centre of the kingdom, Oviedo now becoming the site of his palace. It was this third capital that became the centre of a real renaissance.

In the reign of Alfonso II, Alfonso the Chaste, who came to the throne in 791, the Arabs nevertheless succeeded in sacking the city of Oviedo. But this energetic sovereign, who reigned for over half a century, successfully reconquered part of the Duero valley. He restored the Visigothic palatine Office, contributing to the vitality of a "nationalist" sentiment.

The arts of Asturia

After the period of shocked stupor that followed the defeat at Guadalate, three quarters of a century unfolded before artistic activity was again taken up in the kingdom; Asturian art began to develop after the transfer of the court to Oviedo in 788. This city owes its principal

Miniature from one of the oldest illustrated manuscripts of the "Commentary on the Apocalypse" by the monk Beatus. Conserved in the Royal Library in the Escorial, the book dates from the mid-tenth century and was probably produced at San Millan de la Cogolla in Castile. This illustration deals with the trump sounded by the fourth angel, which destroys a third of the sun, a third of the moon and a third of the stars, while an eagle appears flying in mid-heaven (Library of the Escorial).

monuments to Alfonso II who, to prevent a second sacking of the city like that perpetrated by Abd al-Malik, fortified the new capital; its palace buildings and its main churches were henceforth enclosed in an enceinte wall.

The first work it is essential to include here is a symbol of this little Asturian kingdom: the famous Cross of the Angels, kept in the Camara Santa at Oviedo. This gold votive cross was ordered by Alfonso II and made in 808. Forty-six centimeters (18 inches) across, it has a solid base worked from end to end with filigree, on which polished stones and antique cameos are mounted. This masterpiece of the medieval goldsmith's craft may have been ordered from Carolingian artists, themselves probably inspired by Byzantine works.

Oviedo has the honour, too, of having the largest Spanish church dating from before the Romanesque period, with Santullano, or San Julian de los Prados, 35 metres (115 feet) long. This church was built between 820 and 830, with its three aisles separated from the triple apse by a very high transept. Inside, it bore a polychrome decoration of frescoes inspired by Roman art, representing an architecture of columns and pediments.

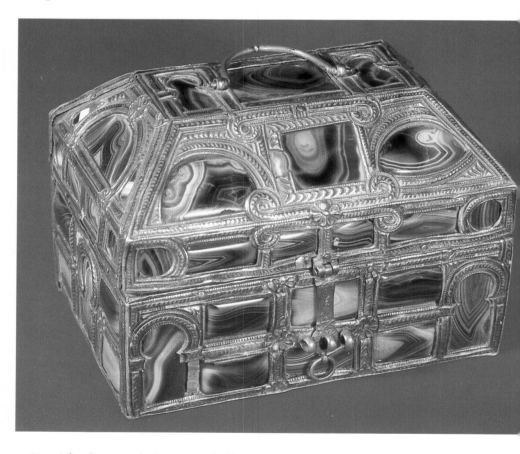

Ivory processional cross dating from 1063, which was given by the king Ferdinand I and Queen Sancha to the monastery of San Isidore de Leon (National Archaeological Museum, Madrid).

Right:
Onyx reliquary, a Mozarab work dating from the tenth century from Oviedo, which was given to the treasure of San Isidore de Leon. The silver setting shows horseshoe arches (at bottom, left and right) which demonstrate its Mozarab manufacture (National Archaeological Museum Madrid).

Outside the royal city, on a hill overlooking the region, king Ramiro I who reigned between 841 and 850 had built, in a place called Naranco, a kind of pleasure villa known today as the Santa María de Naranco. It is of great architectural interest: it consists of one long barrel-vaulted hall announcing the first arrival of the Romanesque style. External buttresses, transverse ribs across the vault and open colonnaded galleries at each end stiffen the structure.

The upward sweep of the building, the lightness of the galleries with their colonnettes and stilted semi-circular arches, are characteristic of architecture under the Ramiros. The same style can be seen again not far away, in the church of San Miguel de Lillo. The entrance to this little sanctuary is decorated with fine bas-reliefs representing a juggler and a lion-tamer with a lion, a theme drawn from the ornament on a sixth-century ivory consular diptych, showing once again that reference back to classical sources which is so much a feature of the Asturian renaissance.

49

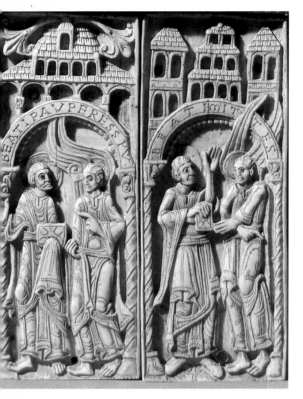

In the same Ramirian style we can point out the little oratory of Santa Cristina de Lena at Vega del Rey, to the south of Oviedo, a work of great originality. Vaulted throughout and with all the emphasis on its height, the nave includes several different levels which give life to the interior space despite its small size. A royal tribune overlooks the entrance, and in front of the choir is a raised "presbytery" including an iconostasis with low walls and arches carved in relief in the Visigothic manner. All these elements make of this tiny Asturian church a jewel of coherence and precision.

Finally a church dating from the time of Alfonso III, Alfonso the Great—San Salvador de Valdedios, built in 893. Here we see the first signs of Mozarab influence in Asturia: there are small windows with twin horseshoe lights surrounded by a frame of the kind called "alfiz" which belongs as much to Christian works as to Moslem but seems to have first emerged around the mihrabs of the mosques in Cordova. Here again, a high vaulted nave buttressed by side aisles is roofed in stone.

Mozarab art

The repopulation of the Duero valley, and particularly of the towns of Leon, Astorga, Burgos and Zamora, in the ninth century marked the arrival of large numbers of Mozarabs in the north. Indeed Leon was to become capital of the kingdom in 913. And it was not far from Leon

The Mozarab church of San Miguel de Escalada near Leon, consecrated in 913. The porch with its horseshoe arches was built in 930. Its twelve arches are perhaps inspired by the twelve gates of the Apocalypse.

Top:
The "Reliquary of the Beatitudes", an ivory casket dating from the end of the Mozarab period in the eleventh century. From the treasure of San Isidore de Leon (National Archaeological Museum, Madrid).

The Mozarab church of San Miguel de Escalada: three aisles separated by two arcades of horseshoe arches on columns of which many are recycled antiques. The ceiling is wooden, unlike those in Ramirian buildings.

that one of the most perfect examples of Mozarab architecture was built: the monastery of San Miguel de Escalada, founded by Alfonso III to receive the monks who had fled from Cordova. The church of this monastery, consecrated in 913 and with a southern portico added in 930, is typified by the horseshoe arches throughout the building. The three apses are even laid out in the form of horseshoe arcs, in place of the square plan of apses in the Visigothic and Asturian churches. The wooden ceiling is supported on elegant arcades with marble columns which are recycled antiques. The partitioned, transparent space of the interior, again with the iconostasis that properly belongs to the mozarab rite, recalls unmistakable, though on a reduced scale, the formulae of the Great Mosque at Cordova.

San Miguel de Escalada also owes its fame to the fact that it was here that the artist-monk, the "archipictor" Magius, produced one of the most famous of the illuminated manuscripts of the Beatus cycle, one of the pinnacles of medieval art in Spain.

The illuminated manuscripts of the "Commentary on the Apocalypse" by Beatus were very popular among the mozarabs: the Revelation of St. John in fact played the role of the central book of the resistance among the Christian communities fighting against Islam. And the Mozarab artists devoted enormous care and effort to illustrating the flamboyant visions of this last book of the Bible. The outcome was a violent art, expressionistic, highly-coloured and wholly original, as

Overleaf (pages 52-53):
Across two pages of Facundus' manuscript of the "Commentary" by Beatus, this illustration, showing the scene from the Relevation in which the woman is menaced by the dragon, counts among the most famous works of Mozarab art. Dating from the mid-eleventh century, with its bands of bright colour, its visionary aspect and its symbolism, it shows the creative power produced among the Christians fighting Islam by the flamboyant text of the Relevation, their Bible of resistance.

witness the twenty-two manuscripts which have come down to us. From the same period of the tenth and eleventh centuries, however, Gospels and Bibles from Spain are extremely rare.

Between the manuscript of the Beatus from the Escorial with its sharp, schematised forms—painted around 950 and one of the oldest known— and the manuscripts of Magius and Facundus with their horizontal bands of bright colour across the illustrations, we can see the development of an expressionistic representation of that world of absolute Good and absolute Evil evoked by St. John in his apocalyptic vision.

Miniature of the "Commentary on the Apocalypse" by Beatus, from the manuscript executed by Facundus in 1047 for Ferdinand I, king of Castile and Leon, and Queen Sancha. On their death they left it to the collegiate church of San Isidore of Leon. It illustrates the passage in the Apocalypse where the angel gives John the Epistle to the church of Ephesus. The architecture represented has a horseshoe arch closed by screen curtains in the Roman style (National Library, Madrid).

51

mulier
amicta sole
et luna sub pedibus
e s. su per capud s
corona stellarū hu
    duode
    cie

serpēns

Romanesque Spain

Detail of a polyptych from the twelfth century showing the three Magi and the Virgin Mary; their faces are in high relief while their bodies are painted flat (Museum of Catalan Art, Barcelona).

The Mozarab era is typified not only by its own specific art, but also by a particular liturgy, a particular emphasis on the Revelation, a calendar counting thirty-eight years more from the birth of Christ than the rest of Christendom, the presence in Toledo of a primate of Spain appointed by the Moslem overlord and therefore obedient to him, and a script of Visigothic origin which is to be found only in Mozarab manuscripts.

Before the Romanesque period, Spain was thus cut off from the rest of Christendom. And, further, a new heresy developed in the territory under Islamic control: Adoptionism, which was effectively a resurgence of the old Visigothic Arianism. This belief, subordinating Christ the Son to God the Father, was supported by the church hierarchy and the primate in Toledo, but was opposed in the kingdom of Asturia, in particular by Beatus, author of the "Commentary on the Apocalypse", who drew strong support from Charlemagne and the Pope. In this context we should bear in mind the role of the Carolingians in the Spanish March, where their presence prepared the birth of the Romanesque, starting first in Catalonia.

The penetration of new ideas into the peninsula was additionally nourished by the development as a place of pilgrimage of Santiago de Compostela, where the tomb of St. James of Galicia was housed. This too contributed to the ending of Spain's particularity. For it was around the question of the liturgy that a struggle of different influences

The church of San Pons at Corbera near Barcelona: an example of the Romanesque art of the eleventh century. The three apses with their Lombard friezes and, above them, the crossing and the rather delicate belltower.

The nave of San Pons de Corbera: dressed stone in irregular courses, powerful arcading with transverse ribs supporting a barrel vault. These are the austere lines of the early Romanesque in Catalonia.

developed in the 11th century which had a major effect on the country. The pressure and influence of the French monastic orders made itself felt through the pilgrimages, and led to the eclipse of the last unorthodox rite within Western Christendom. The Mozarab rite in fact derived from the early Christianity which had survived first among the Visigoths and later among the Christian communities both of independent northern Spain of the occupied region of al-Andalus. It had also contributed to Spanish religious nationalism.

Quite apart from the problems raised by the Adoptionist heresy, the authority of the Pope had remained more or less a dead letter in the ecclesiastical life of Spain from the eighth to the early eleventh centuries. The Benedictine rule had hardly penetrated the monasteries here, and the great majority of the Spanish abbeys were still run according to the rules of the Visigothic age, the rules of St. Isidore, St. Fructuosus and St. Pachomius. The result was a Spanish isolationism based both on the liturgy and on the Moslem presence, and which effectively cut the country off from the rest of Christian Europe.

The Order of Cluny took the lead in the movement which was to put an end to this separatism. The Mozarab rite was first abandoned in

Detail of a painted wooden altar front representing St. Peter and dating from the beginning of the thirteenth century. It is an example of very late Romanesque, already influenced by French Gothic (Museum of Catalan Art, Barcelona).

Christ in glory among the twelve apostles: altar front in painted wood from Seu d'Urgell. There is a clear Byzantine influence in this masterly work of the late twelfth century, perceptible in the treatment of Christ seated as the Pantochrator, and in the yellow backgrounds imitating the gold of Byzantine work (Museum of Catalan Art, Barcelona).

Detail of a panel representing the martyrdom of St. Julitte: a Romanesque wooden altar front from the Boï valley (Museum of Catalan Art, Barcelona).

Aragon and in Catalonia in 1071—both border regions and so susceptible to French influence—but it was not until the time of Pope Gregory VII that the mortal blow was struck against the ancient liturgical customs in the rest of Spain. In Castile it was only progressively, towards the end of the 11th century, that this change took place in the face of a strong reaction from the population. And for a long time the principal text of the Spanish church remained the Mozarabs' most sacred text, the Revelation of St. John.

The old national liturgy was officially abolished by the Council of Burgos in 1080. From then on, the Visigothic script too, which had survived until then in Mozarab manuscripts, was gradually abandoned. In 1090 the Council of Leon ordered the use of the "French" script. But the old writing of the high Spanish Middle Ages survived right up until 1120 in the Cartulary of Sahagun. Finally the Spanish calendar was to disappear in its turn, though it survived here and there right into the 14th century in Spain and even into the 15th century in Portugal. Its abolition in fact did more than just bring the peninsula within the European mainstream; it also erased the last traces of Arianism.

As one can see, the end of the eleventh century marks a programme of

"standardisation" in Spain, with the object of reintegrating the great body of the one and indivisible Church, in which the monastic orders of France carried out a through-going renewal.

The seizure of Toledo

The revival movement that now shook Spain was accompanied by a marked decline in the military power of Islam. In 1009, taking advantage of this weakening on the Moslem side, the Count of Barcelona seized Cordova in an audacious raid. With the end of the caliphate in 1010, state power was divided with the emergence of the Reyes de Taifas, Kings of the Clans, who divided among themselves the spoils of the Umayyad territory. But there was no loss of vivacity in the field of the arts, a fact to which the Aljaferia at Saragossa, for example, bears witness.

Islam was thus considerably weakened, and the Christians were to take advantage of this; on May 25th 1085 Alfonso VI reconquered Toledo. The king had undertaken to leave the Moslems their lives and their

worldly goods, and he carried out his promise. And now, at the same time as the Mozarabs disappear as a specific entity, it is a Mozarab whom the king nominates as governor of the city of Toledo. This man, Sisnando Davidiz, applied a remarkable policy of religious toleration, following the example of the Islamic cities where Christians, Moslems and Jews had coexisted.

The clearest sign of this "standardisation" of the Spanish church was the nomination, in 1086, of the Cluniac monk Bernard de Sédirac as archbishop of Toledo. It was the end of the independence of the church of Toledo, heir to the Arian fathers and home of such heretic movements as Adoptionism: with a Cluniac at its head, the Spanish church re-entered the European fold.

Catalonia, centre of Romanesque art

This period of change, affecting ritual, liturgy, the calendar and ways of thought, was accompagnied by profound changes in the artistic field. This is all the more natural considering that artistic activity was in those

days purely an instrument of religious expression, and made a direct contribution to the liturgy itself. The time of that art which had been specific to the little kingdom of Asturia, like that of the Mozarab monuments around Leon, was now over. With the penetration into Spain of the French religious orders came the breath of the Romanesque world, then in full expansion in the rest of Europe.

The great revival welcomed at the beginning of the 11th century by the monk Raoul Glaber spread by degrees along the pilgrimage route and grew with the monastic communities. As we have seen, it was in Catalonia that the Roman rite was first established and that the reform undertaken under Cluniac direction was begun. From Carolingian times Catalonia, lying as it did on the French border, had escaped the grasp of Toledo and had been in contact with Lombardy and Lotharingia. From Lombardy came the north Italian influences visible in the works of the first Catalonian Romanesque period, similarities that can be seen in the presence of blind arcades and pilasters ("Lombard friezes") in naves that were soon vaulted in stone, with semi-circular apses topped by half-domes, in contrast to the square apses of the churches built in the Visigothic tradition.

Detail of an angel, from San Clemente de Taüll.

On the southern slopes of the Pyrenees, Catalonia in the eleventh century formed a cultural whole with the French provinces of Roussillon and the Cerdagne. Tucked away in their sheltered valleys, hundreds of the monuments of this golden age of Christianity have remained intact, for they lay far from the battlefields of the religious wars and the Revolution. The survival of so many Romanesque churches is also due to Catalonia's isolation from the great revival movements of the colonial era in the sixteenth century—for, elsewhere in Spain, many medieval monuments were demolished to make way for the new styles of the Renaissance and Baroque age.

Among the sanctuaries lost amid the hills we must mention the monastery of San Pons de Corbera, not far from Barcelona. In the eleventh century this was a priory of the Benedictine order, then becoming a daughter establishment of the Cluniac monastery of San Pedro de Casserès. Today only the church is standing. The nave, of great sobriety, is lit only by windows as narrow as arrow-slits. Its barrel-vaulted roof is supported directly by the walls. The very simple crossing built in lantern form marks a transept whose spatial cohesion is quite remarkable. The central apse, flanked by two apsidal chapels, is roofed with a deep semi-dome which must once have born a decoration of frescoes.

The perfect harmony of form and volume, the rhythm of the blind arcades and pilasters, give to San Pons de Corbera a profound serenity which is well conceived in response to the monastery's function as a place of meditation.

Frescoes and statuary

To summon up a picture of the original appearance of the Romanesque churches, whose choirs are now stripped of all decoration, one has only to consider for example the frescoes at San Clemente de Taüll to rediscover the blaze of colour they once bore. For Catalonia is perhaps the region where one may find the greatest number of Romanesque paintings of unequalled quality. At Taüll the great theme spread across

Perched on a summit at an altitude of over 1,000 metres (3,300 feet), the church of San Llorenç del Munt, consecrated in 1064, overlooked a monastic community withdrawn from the world in absolute solitude.

Right:
Interior of the Romanesque church of San Llorenç in Catalonia: an example of the earliest Romanesque style in the Spanish March.

The three apses, with Lombard friezes, form the sturdy chevet of San Llorenç.

the back of the apse is that of the apocalyptic theophanies, the heavenly vision of the four Living Creatures and the twelve apostles surrounding Christ in glory—Christ as the Pantochrator of Byzantine origin.

To this awe-inspiring image of Christ as Alpha and Omega, the beginning and end of all things, the paintings made for altar fronts and the painted wooden statuary offer a profoundly humane complement. Here one finds the compassionate face of the Virgin with the Holy Child as often as the drama of the Passion with crucifixions and calvaries where Christ wears sometimes the serene expression of the King of all peoples and the Son of God, sometimes the overwhelmingly moving face of a man in agony. A work like the descent from the Cross from the church at Taüll marks one of the high points of Romanesque expressionism, at the same time affirming the link between Catalonia and northern Italy.

Even though the churches built by the 11th and 12th century craftsmen are in general quite humble, and use has been made only of local building materials (limestone, left roughly dressed since it was to be plastered to take its decoration of frescoes), and even though they thus bear witness to the austerity of the lives of those communities who gathered in them, their altars carried the sparkling riches of the liturgical articles. These treasures designed for the divine service shone with jewels and enamels.

The belltower of the church rises above this Romanesque cloister in the monastery of Estany in Catalonia, built in the twelfth century. The arcades are supported on pairs of colonnettes with very fine storied capitals.

Capital from the cloister at Estany showing two birds with human heads facing each other across a Tree of Life.

A gallery in the Romanesque cloister of San Cugat del Valles near Barcelona, one of the finest of Catalonian monasteries, dating from the twelfth century. The twin columns are wider spaced than at Estany because of the thick walls required by vaulting in the gallery.

Christ in majesty by Batllo y Batllo: this crucifixion shows Jesus dressed in a rich coloured tunic, and comes from Olot in Gerona province. Mid-twelfth century (Museum of Catalan Art, Barcelona).

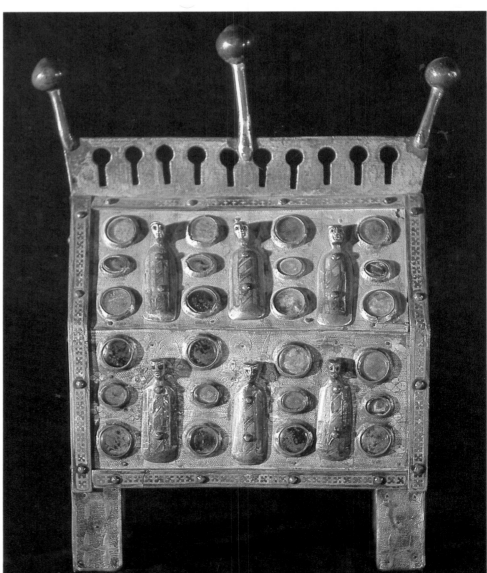

Gilded bronze reliquary with coloured polished stones and enamelled gold angels, dating from the twelfth century (Museum of Catalan Art, Barcelona).

Everywhere, a cult of holy relics has produced admirable reliquaries emblazoned with enamels in brilliant colour, treated with the techniques of cloisonné or of Limousine champlevé. This goldwork was offered to the piety of the faithful for the glorification of God. Nothing was too beautiful to reflect God's splendour, and even those Orders which demanded a vow of poverty did not recoil from such riches designed for the veneration of the Lord, to offer greater majesty and lustre to the realm of the divine. In this jeweller's art where angels alternate with cherubim, every work is testimony to the profound decorative sense of the Romanesque artists and craftsmen. Cut or polished stones sparkle amid gold and silver, glorifying the risen Christ.

The monastery-retreats

These oases of meditation, retreats of knowledge and faith, the monasteries of the Romanesque period where monks incessantly recited the Office, represent the synthesis of medieval civilisation. It was here that Christian culture was reborn after the terrible invasion of the Moor Almanzor which, in 985, had plunged the country into ruin and devastation. Here it was that copyists created magnificently illuminated manuscripts. Here it was that Western music produced its most sublime masterpieces.

Of these cloisters where airy arcades supported by slender colonnettes give rhythm to a space closed in on itself, there is a whole series in Spain worthy of mention. First of all there are Santo Domingo de Silos and San Cugat del Valles with their two-tier porticos, and Santa María de l'Estany with its wealth of carvings. In fact here at Estany, in a monastery dating from the twelfth century, the carving on the corbels of the capitals is not simply a decoration; it provides a kind of "poor man's Bible", making the Good Word and the praise of the Lord accessible to all the faithful, literate and illiterate alike, by means of images.

Descent from the cross, from the church of Santa María de Taüll: this monumental sculpture of the late twelfth century, in wood which must originally have been painted, achieves an impressive expressionism full of pathos, together with a realism that conveys a solemn nobility (Museum of Catalan Art, Barcelona).

Nativity painted on a wooden altar front, from the early thirteenth century. This detail, from a large panel from Avila, shows Byzantine influences (Museum of Catalan Art, Barcelona).

Virgin and child in painted wood dating from the twelfth century, attributed to the painter of the altar front at Santa María de Taüll. It is a major work of Catalan wood carving, expressive of the peaceful majesty of the Romanesque (National Archaeological Museum, Madrid).

It is within these monastery walls that the art of painting on wood was born, marvellous examples of which can be seen spanning the 11th to the 13th centuries. In this field too Catalonia holds a special place, for while there is an almost total absence of these paintings elsewhere in Christian Europe, here the Museum of Catalan Art in Barcelona alone has assembled dozens of masterpieces. The most varied influences can be seen in them: from France, Italy and even from Byzantium, influences the Catalan painters have fused into an original style of their own.

Through the power of their colouring, the sureness of their line, the audacity of their spatial arrangements and their juxtaposition of colours applied flat to the wood, these paintings, designed to decorate altar fronts, reredos, baldachins, crucifixes and reliquaries reach the summit of accomplishment. All the themes of the Christian message have been called upon, from Nativity scenes and the childhood of Christ to the Resurrection and the Revelation. But the lives of the saints take pride of

place, as paradigms for imitation by the faithful. And the pages of the thirteenth century hagiography brought together in the "Golden Legend" are illustrated here too, telling of the exemplary lives of the Church Fathers or the heroic deaths of the martyrs. It is a whole iconography reflecting the popular preoccupations of the medieval world and the spiritual climate of the Romanesque age.

The pilgrimages of St. James

Faith in the legend according to which St. James the Apostle brought Christianity to Spain drew the pilgrims of St. James to Santiago in Galicia and contributed to an exchange of knowledge and culture, and the spread of new ideas in Spain. Known as the "camino francés", the "road of the French", the pilgrimage route stretched from central France to the western extremity of the Iberian peninsula. This pilgrimage became the equal of that which had once led to Jerusalem, but which had been rendered impossible by the arrival in the Holy City of the Seljuk Turks, whose presence there had provoked the Crusades. For many of the faithful the road of St. James was a substitute for the road to Jerusalem.

Detail of the door of a reliquary, offset with ivory reliefs. A late Romanesque work, it already shows the elongated figures typical of Gothic art (National Archaeological Museum, Madrid).

Left:
A very lovely reliquary in Limousine enamel, with an ornament of twelve angels in relief. Champlevé enamel on the gilded bronze reflects the richness of Romanesque liturgical articles (Museum of Catalan Art, Barcelona).

Top:
Detail of St. John the Baptist painted on an altar front of the early thirteenth century, from Gesera (Huesca), in which a late Romanesque artist has represented the visionary aspect of St. John (Museum of Catalan Art, Barcelona).

The whole length of this road to Compostela was dotted with churches, monasteries (in which the cult of precious relics developed), hostelries, inns, staging-posts. Santiago, at the end of the long trail, was endowed with a sumptuous five-aisled basilica essentially built by craftsmen and artists from France. Begun in 1077 work continued until 1089 and was then renewed in 1125 when the building of the Portico de la Gloria was begun. We know the name of one sculptor who worked on this doorway around 1188: Master Mathieu. This craftsman, probably a pupil of the school of Saint-Denis in France, created, within a framework which is still typically Romanesque and retains a rigorously semi-circular arch, a work which announces the finest art of the dawn of the Gothic age, as at Chartres or Saint-Denis.

The Romanesque works of Old Castile, meanwhile, such as one may see in Segovia, are typified by their perfectly dressed stonework, their rather dry carvings and their somewhat heavy forms. The churches have kept to the Mozarab tradition of lateral porticos such as we have seen at San Miguel de Escalada. In Segovia these porticos flank the churches of San Juan de los Caballeros and San Millan (1110) as well as those of San Martin and San Estaban, whose 13th-century five-storey tower has a particularly proud elegance and is suggestive, in its vertical upsweep, of the Gothic style.

In Leon, which remained until 1230 the capital of the united kingdoms of Castile and Leon, Ferdinand I built the Royal Pantheon, consecrated in 1049; then in 1060 the emir Almotamid gave the body of

The very fine belltower of the Romanesque period on the church of San Esteban, Segovia, dating from the thirteenth century. It has been called the "queen of Spanish towers".

Right:
Romanesque gallery with storied capitals in the church of San Esteban, Segovia. From the end of the twelfth century, it is a good example of the lateral porches so specific to the architecture of this region of Castile.

St. Isidore to the king and it was brought to the Pantheon. In the narthex of this high place of Christian Spain, the collegiate church of San Isidore the tombs of the kings were placed, under vaults painted with storied frescoes. The church also housed a famous treasure; and among the pieces which have given it its renown we should mention the remarkable chalice of Doña Urraca, daughter of Ferdinand I. Doña Urraca's chalice is among the masterpieces of the Romanesque goldsmith's craft. It was placed in the basilica in 1063, and is composed of two antique onyx cups mounted top to bottom with goldwork. A wide border enhanced with filigree, cut and polished stones and a large knot at the centre, this too decorated with filigree work in which is spelled out its donor's name, makes up a piece one could describe as baroque in spirit, and which announces, though still a little crudely, the mountings with antique elements so loved by Abbott Suger of Saint-Denis.

A spirit of unity

It would certainly be presumptuous to think we could evoke here the prodigious diversity of the provinces of Romanesque Spain—Navarra, Aragon, Castile, Leon, Galicia—by mentioning just a few works, some of them lesser works but which have remained more authentic than the great sanctuaries reworked and enriched ten times over in the Gothic, Renaissance and Baroque periods.

But what typifies this Romanesque Spanish art is its abundance, its inventiveness, its constant renewal, as one may see in the innumerable different solutions applied to architectural problems, in vaulting and in decoration as well as at the structural level. And despite this multiplicity, the style remains profoundly unitary: it reflects a coherent world in which the same sacred vision has drawn together the buildings of the whole northern part of the peninsula on the one hand, liberated from the Moslem yoke, and the works of France, Italy, the Rhineland and the Alps on the other. Through its art, Christian Europe forms a single entity. And this period, divided up as it was by the feudal powers, nevertheless developed a true unity of faith and of thought.

And with one effort of force, this Christian community which "decked itself in a white coat of churches" now launched eastwards to liberate Jerusalem and the Holy Places, and southwards across the Spanish peninsula in the great thrust of the Reconquest.

Part of the treasure of San Isidore de Leon, the chalice of Doña Urraca, daughter of Ferdinand I and Queen Sancha, who presented it to the collegiate church in 1063. It is enriched with polished stones and intaglio work in Romanesque style. The goldwork mounting holds two antique onyx cups (Treasure of San Isidore de Leon).

The famous Portico de la Gloria in the cathedral of Santiago de Compostela. Within a structure which is still Romanesque, characterised by its semi-circular arches and dating back to 1125, the French craftsman Master Mathieu working between 1168 and 1188 has created sculptures which already bring the first breath of the Gothic style.

The Reconquest and the Gothic Age

In Spain the Gothic age is also the time of the epic of the Reconquista and the time of the cathedral builders. Under the impulse of currents coming from France, from the Cistercian Order and the great builders in the ogival style on the one hand, and from the influx of knights and lords from across the Pyrenees who came to seek their fortunes in the newly liberated territories on the other, Christian Spain was to undertake these two great enterprises simultaneously.

Drawing on eleventh-century developments in the military, social, economic and artistic fields, the kingdoms of Castile, Leon, Aragon and Portugal made tremendous progress in the 12th and 13th centuries. The territorial gains of the Christian armies during this period were more lasting and less threatened by sudden offensives on the part of the Moslem armies. Soon, the advance of the Reconquista became irreversible.

The phases of the Reconquest

From the time of the collapse and partition of the caliphate of Cordova in the early eleventh century, and above all after the siezure of Toledo in 1085 by Alfonso VI, the Reconquista became a motive force and a leitmotiv for all the Hispanic kings. This first great success which ended in taking back a whole emirate from the Moors—and with it,

View of the walled city of Avila in Castile, from the south-west: one can see the twelfth-century ramparts on Roman foundations. These walls, 2,400 metres (2,600 yards) long, the curtain wall dotted with semi-circular towers at 20 to 25-metre (22 to 27-yard) intervals, offer the finest example of Spanish military architecture.

Left:
View along the towers of the ramparts at Avila, with battlements at the top and the foundations resting on the bare rock.

Facing page, top:
During the Reconquista, castles sprang up all over Christian Spain as feudal lords sought refuge from the Arab raids. This well-preserved little Gothic fortress stands guard over a pass on the road from Toledo to Avila, near Talavera de la Reina.

Facing page, bottom:
That symbol of the spirit of the Reconquista, the adventures of Don Quixote de la Mancha battling with windmills, might have taken place on this Cresteria Manchega above Consuegra, where windmills surround a Gothic fortress built on the ruins of a Roman castrum.

moreover, a city which had been the capital of the Visigothic kingdom and which therefore had considerable symbolic importance for the Christians—had been a great encouragement.

But in 1086 just after these events, summoned by their co-religionists in Spain, the Almoravids, Berbers from North Africa, disembarked and defeated the Christian knights at Zalacca. They left as soon as they had saved the emirs of Seville and Granada, but in 1100 returned to Spain and in the space of a few years seized the whole of the southern region held by the Moslems, whom they considered to have betrayed the cause of Islam in accepting the overlordship of the Christian kings.

We should make it clear that in this period the Iberian peninsula was not split into two monolithic rival regions with the Christians on one side and the Moslems on the other. The antagonism of the eighth to tenth centuries had given way by now to a certain accommodation. Areas of entente multiplied, as did reciprocal influences. The "frontiers" were altogether permeable. Emirs were to be seen fighting alongside the knights against other Moslems, and Christian kings drawing up pacts with Islamic chiefs over whom they exercised a kind of suzerainty.

The Christians were limited by no frontier as a front line in the fight for the Christian faith against the Islamic world. There were buffer zones, fluctuating frontiers. Spain was not only the scene of armed confrontation but equally a region in which fruitful dialogue was held, especially in the commercial and cultural fields. Even during the periods of open war, positions were never entrenched. The feudal system which was progressively established in the Christian zone raised echoes in the Moslem areas—and proved itself stronger than religious antagonisms.

But the sense of an irreconcilable opposition between Christ's faithful

Unfolding like a comic strip, the illustrations of the "Cantigas de Santa María" by Alfonso the Wise; six miniatures, each about 10 centimetres (4 inches) square, on each page 50 centimetres by 33 (20 inches by 13). This 43rd story of the "Cantigas" tells how the count Don García defeated the Moors with the aid of the Virgin Mary.

This much enlarged detail of the fourth miniature from Cantiga XLIII shows Christain knights during the battle: helmets, shields, coats of mail, swords and standards show with great precision the armaments of the thirteenth century.

and those of Mohammed remained lively, and indeed it was during this period that the concept of the Infidel emerged. The Almoravids replaced the tolerance of the Umayyad era by a hard and fast Islam: the Christians of al-Andalus suffered persecutions and deportations. And at the intellectual level the Berbers rejected the heritage of Graeco-Roman thought, on which the caliphate had drawn considerably in the sciences and philosophy; it was now considered ill-omened.

And the conflict was exacerbated now; the Castilian and Aragon kings seized Saragossa in 1118 and then, in 1146, Almeria. The rapid decline of the Almoravids, who succumbed to a taste for luxury and refinement, led to the intervention in Spain of yet another Berber power from Morocco: the Almohads who set out to rebuild the Almoravid empire, succeeded in retaking Almeria and rallied the last of the emirs.

A further detail from the same miniature of Cantiga XLIII, showing the Moorish troops, among whom can be seen a turbaned Arab, a negro and Christian knights. One can see that the Reconquista was not a religious war between Christians and Moslems but a feudal struggle in which the knights chose the camp which best served their interests.

Detail of a miniature from the Cantigas, number XXVIII, showing the siege of Constantinople when it was seized by the crusaders in 1204. Crossbowmen cover the sappers as they work protected by huge shields forming a "tortoise"; and on the left a ballista, the military engine inherited from the Romans.

Pressure from the Christian forces did not let up. Only the defeat at Alarcos made the Castilians feel themselves once again under threat. But at the time of this battle the Almohads were in alliance with the Christians of Leon—a demonstration of the degree to which the adversaries' interests overlapped.

It was with the victory of the Christians at Las Navas de Tolosa in 1212 that the great last phase of the Reconquista began, launched simultaneously by Castile, Aragon and Portugal. 1232 marked the taking of Baleares; 1236 the fall of Cordova; 1246 that of Seville. In 1252 Alfonso X, Alfonso the Wise, came to the throne and the Christian advance reached its furthest limits with the seizure of Cadiz. From this point on all that was left of al-Andalus was the kingdom of Granada, where the last Moslem sovereigns of Spain were to reign until 1492.

The fine sexpartite vaults of the refectory in the monastery of Santa María de Huerta, built in 1215 in the Burgundian style. A Cistercian work, lit by six tall Gothic lancet windows, this hall is one of the finest works of the thirteenth century.

The "Cantigas" of Alfonso the Wise

Son of Ferdinand III or Saint Ferdinand, king of Castile and Leon, and of Beatrice of Swabia, Alfonso X was born in Toledo in 1221. This fact was of capital importance for the whole direction of his thinking. For during its Arab period Toledo had been a centre of high culture where Moslems, Jews and Christians lived together quite harmoniously. And this model of tolerance lay deep in the king's philosophy.

Alfonso X was thirty-one when he came to the throne. He bore the title of "King of the Romans and Emperor", an epithet which speaks volumes for his dream of restoring Charlemagne's empire and through that the empire of Rome—a nostalgic dream of all the great medieval kings.

Even before coming to power, Alfonso had distinguished himself in all the main disciplines of the knowledge of his times: he was poet, musician, historian, legislator and astronomer at the same time. For the Spanish peninsula in the thirteenth century was a focal point of Gothic learning. In 1248 the future king called together the most famous Chris-

The north gallery of the Cistercian Gothic cloister of the monastery of Santa María de Poblet, built in the thirteenth century. With its clustered pillars, its capitals without any figurative decoration, its gemel windows and its vaulting with intersecting ribs, this cloister bears a profoundly contemplative imprint.

The magnificent fountain for the monks' ablutions, in the monastery garden at Santa María de Poblet. Although the semi-circular arches are still Romanesque, the ribs, the colonnettes and the well-lit space already denote the Gothic imprint on this late twelfth century building.

tian, Jewish and Moslem thinkers in astronomy; from this commission the famous "Alphonsine Tables" were established.

It was openness of spirit—right in the heat of the Reconquista and the crusades—that earned Alfonso X his renown as a man of wisdom. His library of 250 volumes, considerable for those times, included classical, Arab and Christian writers, and Alfonso also ordered translations into Latin of the Koran, the Talmud and some works of the Cabala; yet, for all that, he was a fervent Christian.

This royal poet and musician was the author of that masterpiece of Iberian Gothic work, the famous "Cantigas de Santa María". This is a collection of pious texts, written in the Galician language (from which modern Portuguese derives), recounting miracles of the Virgin Mary in

Facing page:
The north window in the chevet of Leon cathedral, dating from the end of the thirteenth century. The wall has become a wall of coloured light, thanks to the stained glass techniques imported from France, where this craft was at its apogee.

The cathedral of Santa María de Regla at Leon, its ground plan borrowed from Rheims and its front elevation from Amiens, by the architect Guillaume de Rouen. The three great west doors, decorated with statues of the saints, are flanked by towers; the tower on the right was completed only in the fifteenth century.

the poetic tradition of the troubadours and minstrels. Inspired by the "Book of Miracles of St. Mary of Rocamadour", these texts recount various legends centred around miraculous interventions by the Mother of Christ, to whom the Gothic age, with its profound need for a humanisation of the divine, devoted a particularly fervent cult.

This naive piety may seem surprising in a man of erudition, but in fact it was a typical characteristic of the thirteenth century mentality. Knowledge and mystic fervour could quite well co-exist. For if the simple religious spirit of these "Cantigas" is closer to the faith of the unlettered than to a reasoned conviction like that of his great contemporary St. Thomas Aquinas (1225-1274), this is precisely because Alfonso has retained intact the medieval spirit of thought.

These poems to the Virgin were meant to be sung, and we also still have the musical notations for them. These are short pieces belonging to the secular monodic style of the French troubadours of the thirteenth century, though some of the songs have been influenced too by the music of the Mozarabs, and have made use of forms and musical instruments that come from the Moslem tradition.

There are several manuscripts of the "Cantigas" extant. The most

The Puerta del Pardón, main door of the cathedral at Toledo, with its richly carved ornamentation (fifteenth century).

Top:
The fine Gothic nave of Toledo cathedral. This is a very pure style, from the first half of the thirteenth century, and with no triforium. The lovely Flamboyant rose window closing the nave to the west gives onto a fifteenth-century façade.

Facing page, bottom:
Interior of the cathedral in Seville, with its five aisles in the Gothic style begun in 1420.

remarkable is that at the Escorial; this is a monumental work of Gothic illumination. The great folio contains no less than 1257 miniatures, beneath which run the words of the songs. It is the most extensive evidence we possess of daily life in the Iberian peninsula in this Gothic age of the thirteenth century.

Each page is divided into six miniatures with one complete story, like a comic strip. The illustrations themselves show an extraordinary variety of settings: some of the stories take place in a church or in the manor house of a lord, others in a merchant's shop, others again beneath the walls of a town under siege, or out in the countryside. In them we can see the supper table of a lord, a Jewish money-changer's house, a field of battle or Christian ships assailed by Moorish galleys. We see all the characters of the time, from king to serf, not forgetting knights, churchmen, merchants, musicians, jugglers, sculptors. The details are a wealth of information about all aspects of life from the arts of war and weaponry to musical instruments and furniture. The lives of the great and the poor in their entirety come alive through this masterpiece, in a style that shows clearly the influence of the French Gothic art of illumination.

The Gothic style

The penetration of the Gothic style in Spain always met with a surprising inertia, even resistance, in the country areas. The population in effect regarded these forms as something foreign and for a long time preferred the old Romanesque style which still flourished even in the remotest valleys. In the villages of the Aragon and Castilian kingdoms building kept to the Romanesque pattern right into the fourteenth century.

The Gothic style carries a vertical thrust even more marked than in the tallest of the Romanesque churches. Typical of the Gothic are its vaults with intersecting ribs over the naves, its use of clustered piers taking the weight of the vaults' groins, the introduction of the flying buttress to counteract the thrust of the vault and a lightening of the structure, stemming from a search for light and reflected in the opening of ever larger windows to the point where the outer walls of the building are almost entirely replaced by glass. The stained glass in the windows is as brightly coloured as had been Romanesque frescoes. These

Masterpiece of late Gothic, this altarpiece from the cathedral in Seville, which stands in the Capilla Mayor, was made between 1482 and 1526 by a Flemish sculptor named Dancart and his Spanish Pupils.

Sculptures on the door jamb of the Puerta del Nacimiento, dating from the fifteenth century, in the Gothic cathedral in Seville.

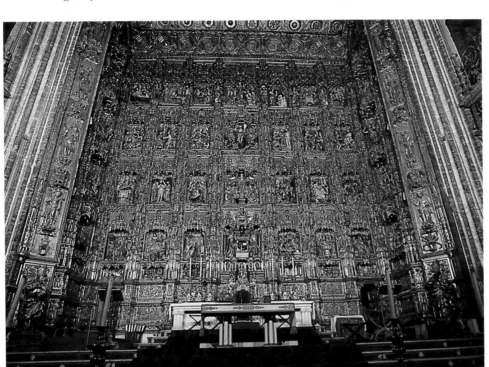

characteristics however are the mark of a pure Gothic at the peak of its maturity, and such examples remain relatively rare in the Iberian peninsula where they always appear as something imported, fruit of the actions of kings and lords rather than of any popular aspiration.

The Gothic vault, however, with its pointed arches and its intersecting ribs, was very widely adopted in Spain; one frequently sees Gothic vaults serving as the roofing structure of buildings which otherwise retain a Romanesque layout and structure, and remain dark, mystery having been regarded as essential to a place of prayer or meditation.

It was the spread of Cistercian monasteries in Spain during the twelfth century that introduced and propagated the Gothic style. The Cistercian Order was based at Cîteaux in Burgundy, an offshoot of the Benedictine Order. Its daughter houses in Spain included some famous monastic centres, in particular Santa María de Huerto in the Saragossa region, founded in 1162, and Santa María de Poblet in the Tarragona region, founded in 1153.

In these two Cistercian monasteries one may follow the evolution that marks the progressive adoption of Gothic forms in the context of a Romanesque tradition. Thus at Poblet one of the galleries of the cloister is still constructed with semi-circular arches and the communal fountain is Romanesque in form, while the three other galleries of the cloister were built, in the thirteenth century, with pointed arches, piers like clusters of attached columns, and vaults with intersecting ribs.

At Huerta, particularly notable is the extraordinary Gothic hall of the monks' refectory, built in 1215 in a very pure Burgundian style, with sexpartite vaults of remarkable lightness and daylight pouring through six tall lancet windows.

Gothic triptych representing the Crucifiction, the Annunciation, and apostles and saints. It is 62 centimetres (24 inches) high and comes from the province of Saragossa; probably the work of an ivory carver from the School of Paris, it dates from the fourteenth century (National Archaeological Museum, Madrid).

Cathedrals in the French style

The erection of Gothic cathedrals in the principal cities of Spain—Toledo, Burgos, Leon, Barcelona, Avila, Salamanca, Seville and Segovia—was an act of government as much as an act of piety. For the nobility it was a question of marking its convergence both with the ideal of the Crusade preached by the French monastic orders and with the new philosophical and religious view of the world and the universe within the

Ivory diptych representing scenes from the Passion, by craftsmen from the School of Paris in the fourteenth century (National Archaeological Museum, Madrid).

feudal system. The art of the time expresses a consciously adopted social and political position.

So Gothic art arrives as if parachuted into Spanish towns, and does not, as in France, spring from common aspirations. And, as in Toledo for example, the cathedral sometimes remained the only ogival building in the town for many years. The movement was not necessarily followed at a popular level: neither public buildings not the manor houses of the nobility were inspired by Gothic forms.

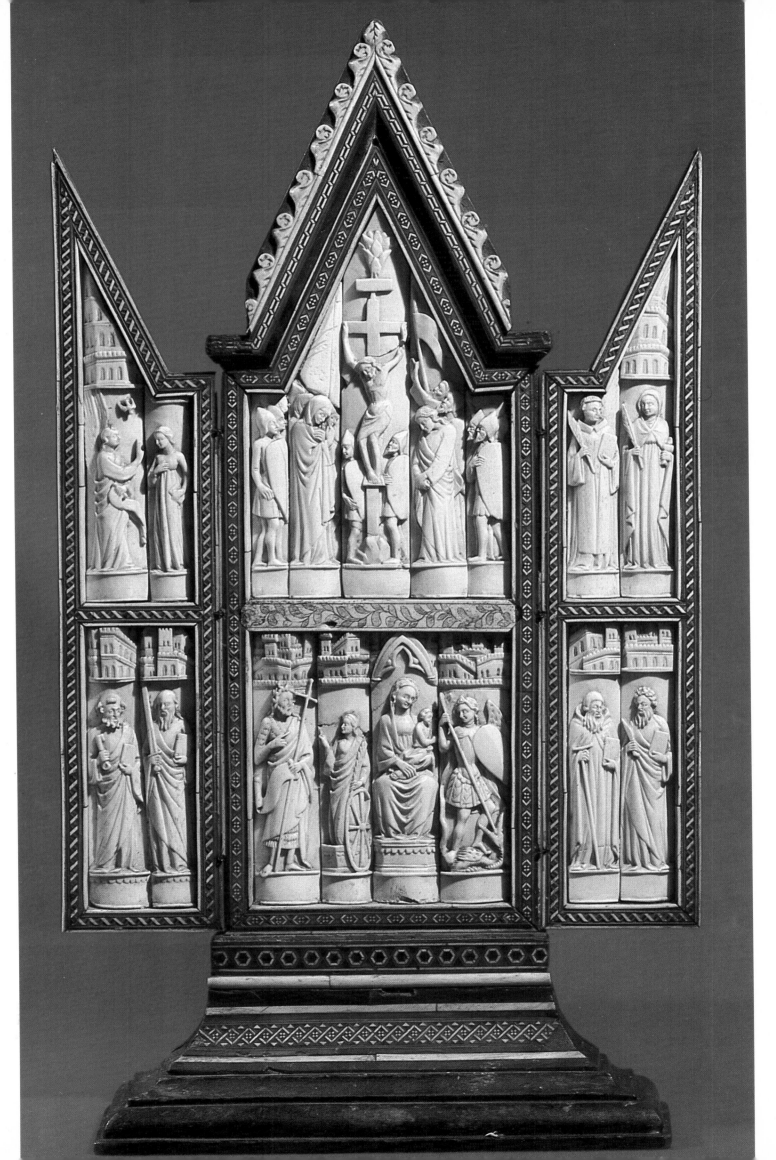

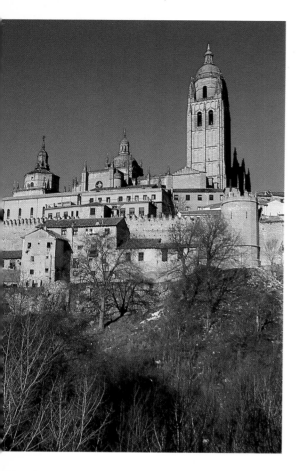

Two views of Segovia cathedral overlooking the old Castilian town. The chevet in the Gothic Flamboyant style with the pinnacles above shows it is a late Gothic work: it was begun in 1522.

Burgos, capital of Castile, was endowed with a cathedral whose foundations were laid in 1221 and which was already consecrated in 1230 in an unfinished state. Work on it continued for three centuries, and the end product is certainly one of the finest Gothic works in all Spain.

Also founded by Ferdinand III, Toledo's cathedral was begun in 1227. It was to play the rôle of a standard flying over the city which stood out as a forward bastion of the Reconquest. It is a dark building with five aisles, in a very pure Gothic style, its lines relatively stocky and yet elegant. Building work was only completed around 1500, not counting the many later additions. It was a master mason of French origin who supervised the work on it for fifty years during the thirteenth century; he also taught the Gothic techniques in a workshop in the town.

In Leon, capital of the kingdom that bore its name, work began on the cathedral in 1255, on a layout which is that of Rheims cathedral on a reduced scale, while its front elevation is clearly inspired by that at Amiens. The windows, especially those in the choir, which occupy the whole width of the walls between the piles of the structure, form a continuous wall of glass, producing a building that is all light and transparency, reminiscent of the Sainte-Chapelle in Paris.

The final brilliance of the Gothic age

Marked by civil wars, the fourteenth century also saw in Spain the ravages of the Great Companies; then plague and famine decimated the population of Castile. The progress that had soared across centuries kept up its momentum only in Aragon and Catalonia, with an expansion in the Mediterranean regions which gave Barcelona and Majorca the means to develop and pursue the policies of greatness they aspired to.

Huge cathedrals and churches were built, and at the same time royal palaces and castles in the Flamboyant style sprang up, showing the adoption of Gothic forms for secular architecture. This is particularly the case in the Ayuntamiento in Barcelona (1369).

Further, in the 15th century the construction of Seville cathedral

between 1402 and 1519 by French architects shows northern influence still spreading through the reconquered territories. This huge cathedral was built on the former site of the town's great mosque, partly destroyed in an earthquake. It is connected in a most original way to those parts of the Moslem structure that had been preserved. Thus the patio, previously the courtyard of the twelfth-century Almohad edifice, and the bell-tower, which is quite simply the old minaret with two storeys added for the belfry, have been preserved in the reconstruction.

But the most surprising work of this last phase of the Gothic style is perhaps Segovia cathedral; the fact that it was built, with its pinnacles surrounding a chevet in the Flamboyant style, as late as the mid-sixteenth century, makes it a remarkable survival. Only the side door, worked in the style of the Escorial, and the high cupola above the transept, 67 metres (220 feet) at its summit, reflect the spirit of the Renaissance. Still in the town of Segovia, the picturesque fourteenth-century castle of el Alcazar offers an example of military architecture adapted in the fifteenth century to the life of the royal court as king Juan II of Castile conceived it.

Thus for over 350 years, the spirit of a Gothic art born in France was progressively adapted to the Spanish character, to shine in its later works with a very particular brilliance that distinguishes them from their French models. For in France, while in 16th-century work such as Saint-Eustache in Paris is still within the spirit of the Middle Ages, the dawn of the Renaissance which broke in Italy in the 13th century had already reached Aragon with the popes. At the end of the 15th century this new spirit already showed its spark in the Casa de los Conchas an Salamanca and in the sculpture of Gil de Siloe, which clearly shows the imprint of Italy. The Gothic age was now over, and in 1501 the Royal Hospital at San Juan de Compostela inaugurated the Plateresque style.

The Mudejars and the Kingdom of Granada

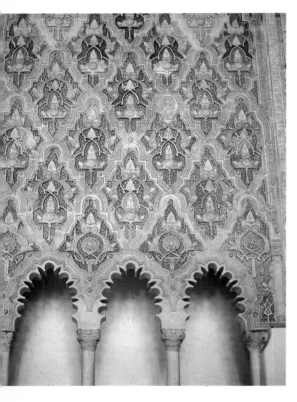

In the reconquered territories of Spain, the Moslem presence which had lasted for between five and seven hundred years depending on the region had given birth to a whole Hispano-Mauresque population who spoke the Arabic language, followed the Islamic faith and had developed their own refined culture. This society which had for twenty to thirty generations shaped the majority of the population of the southern part of Spain, alongside the Jews and the Mozarabs, now fell into the hands of the Christians in the aftermath of the victorious wars of the Reconquista.

These Arabic-speaking Moslems, now living under the rule of Christian feudal lords and of the kings of Castile or Aragon, these were the Mudejars. The existence of the Mudejars is one of the most curious and revelatory aspects of the specificity of Spanish civilisation. In fact it is one example of that religious tolerance of which the seizure of Toledo in the days of Alfonso the Wise had already given proof.

The status of the Mudejars, similar to that of the Mozarabs during the Islamic era, was that of tributaries obliged to pay a series of taxes, and in particular a capitation tax, but free to practice their own religion, language and customs. In the recently-conquered southern provinces the Mudejars constituted the great majority of the population, and they also had their own art and forms of expression. It was an art expressive of a way of life of great refinement which soon seduced the conquerors. The new lords often adopted, along with a Mudejar workforce, the

Sculpted plaster decoration and multifoil arches in the synagogue of El Transito in Toledo, dating from 1366. This is a typical example of Toledan Mudejar art.

The oldest synagogue in Toledo dates from 1180, was rebuilt in the thirteenth century, and is known today as the Santa María la Blanca, having been transformed into a church in 1405. It is built in the style of the Almohad mosques, with five aisles and horseshoe arches.

fashions and customs of their Moslem vassals. In Seville for example we may see Peter I, Peter the Cruel, have his Mudejar artists and architects build a sumptuous palace within the very walls of the Alcazar, a palace which demonstrates the extreme delicacy of Andalusian life. Once again history shows us victors conquered by the high culture of the vanquished...

Apart from this, just as some Mozarabs had learned Arabic, the Reconquista accelerated the interpenetration of the two communities and the Romance tongues continued to co-exist with the language of the Koran. Mudejar craftsmen worked on the construction of churches and monasteries. Many belltowers, especially in Aragon, show a technology and a decoration of directly Moorish origin even though they are post-Reconquista works.

The Mudejar contribution

It is in Toledo, first among the big cities with a strong Mudejar majority, that we can see the effects of the new symbiosis. The Puerta del

The dome of the Capilla Real, the Chapel Royal, built in 1258 within the hypostyle of the Great Mosque at Cordova. The work is in the Mudejar style, and was built by order of Alfonso X. Scalloped arches intersect amid delicate stalactite motifs.

Sol, dating from the fourteenth century, where the military building techniques of Arabs and Christians are combined, and the lovely church of Santiago del Arrabal, a thirteenth century work, both show the Mudejar contribution in decoration and craftsmanship.

From the same period, a synagogue today known as the Santa María la Blanca and which stands in the old Jewish district of Toledo, offers the paradox of a Jewish religious building constructed by Moslem workmen. The sanctuary has been inspired by the layout of an Almohad mosque, with five aisles of horseshoe arcades and capitals with interlacing designs offset by pine cones on octagonal masonry pillars. The other synagogue that has survived in Toledo, El Transito, built in 1366 for Samuel Levi, treasurer to Peter the Cruel, has preserved its carved and painted stucco decoration, enhanced by Hebrew inscriptions. It is a kind of panel decoration equally characteristic of the art of the Moorish palaces of Granada built under the Nasrid sovereigns.

In the Great Mosque at Cordova, reconsecrated to the Christian religion after the Reconquista in 1236, Alfonso the Wise had the Capilla Real built by Mudejars. The decoration of this Chapel Royal, and particularly its cupola with interlaced multifoil arches covered with subtly-worked stalactites, is of the most delicate and masterful skill. This raised chapel later served as a pantheon, and was plundered in the days of Ferdinand IV and of Alfonso XI.

In the field of palace architecture, it is in Seville that Mudejar work reaches its apogee, with the construction of the palace of Peter the Cruel. This complex, built in 1364 in the heart of the old Andalusian fortress of the Alcazar, founded in 712, has a patio called the Patio de las Doncellas which is of the most airy lightness. Here the multifoil arches stand within an ogival layout, marking a fusion of the Moorish and Gothic formulae, and are supported on paired colonnettes of great delicacy.

The decoration in a mosaic of faïence or "azulejos", in star-shaped geometric motifs, the pierced stucco-work and the polychrome, the tortuous passageways full of surprises, the richness and luxury of this palace make it a marvel of Andalusian art. Its original balance was to be upset by the addition, in the sixteenth century, of an upper floor with galleries.

But it is in the great Ambassadors' Salon that Mudejar decoration reaches the summit of its prolific richness. Supported on pendentives covered in stalactites, a cupola was erected in 1420 over this hall which must previously have been covered simply by a panelled ceiling. Here cockle-shells appear, mixing Christian symbols with the Moslem themes of the decoration.

The great Salon of the Ambassadors in the Alcazar at Seville: testimony to the luxury of Mudejar art in the days of Peter the Cruel: here cockle shells introduce a Christian theme among the typically Moorish decoration of gilded and painted stucco.

The Nasrid kingdom of Granada

Last stronghold of Islam in Spain, the kingdom of Granada became the retreat of all those Moslems who refused to live under Christian suzerainty. It was to form a kind of bastion of the faith. There was now a radicalisation of the methods of government in this Nasrid dynasty which ruled between 1230 and 1492: tolerance gave way to a fastidious rigidity and to a strict observance of the Koranic precepts. No Mozarab might live in this small kingdom crouched against the Sierra Nevada. The more the Moslem power was threatened, the more reviled was the very name of Christianity.

From now on scientific and philosophical speculation gave way to commentaries on the law, mystic writings, and integrist thought. The country stiffened, in a last effort of will, into an attitude about which we should have no illusions: what haunts it is the prospect of its own fate. This tended, too, to an increase in the refinement of the arts—forms become all grace, in curious contrast to a certain military rigour. This is precisely the paradox reflected in the palaces of this dynasty, where delicate earthly paradises are enclosed in powerful defensive walls.

Facing page, top:
The Casa de Pilatos, Pilate's House, a fifteenth century building in Seville, mixes Mudejar and Renaissance styles.

Facing page, bottom:
The Patio of the Ladies in the Alcazar in Seville, built for the king Peter the Cruel, whose palace dates from 1364 and was reworked in the late fifteenth century for the Catholic Kings. This patio is among the masterpieces of Mudejar art. With its airy porticos in which fine colonnettes hold up multifoil arches, and its central fountain, the building reflects all the seductive grace of that refined lifestyle of the Moorish dynasties.

This is the fountain, resting on twelve stone lions, which gave its name to the Court of the Lions in the Alhambra in Granada. At the far end, the door opens into the Hall of the Abencerrajes with its stalactite dome.

The defensive walls of the Alhambra, the Red Citadel, in Granada. The foundations go back to the eleventh century, but the walls were restored in 1230 with the arrival of the Nasrid dynasty.

Bird's eye view of the Court of the Lions in the Alhambra, Granada, built by Mohammed V in 1354.

The palace complex of the Alhambra in Granada, which has come down to us miraculously intact, partly due to the respect paid to it by the Catholic Kings when they entered the city, expresses very well the full potential of an art which is precious to the point of affectation. It is brought home to one that this is secular architecture reproducing all the characteristics of the Almoravid works, and nourished by the same sources as the mosques and madrasas of Morocco such as may still be seen in Marrakesh and Fez. In structure and in decoration: in the use of courtyards with fountains and tinkling water (for Mohammed often spoke of water to evoke the joys of the faithful in paradise): in the lofty porticos, their shade so welcoming as a shelter from the blinding sun, and where one may walk under scalloped or multifoil arches held up by slender colonnettes: or in the tiny stalactites that cover the cupolas, this late architecture of the Moslem Far West forms a coherent stylistic unity.

The foundations of the towers and defensive walls around the Alhambra, the Red Fortress, date back to the eleventh century, but it was not until three hundred years later that the palace itself saw the light of day. The palace is built up around two courtyards placed at right angles to each other, producing an L-shaped layout. Around these two open spaces are spread out the royal apartments, the baths, reception halls and gardens.

The oldest of these courtyards, the Court of the Myrtles or the "Alberca", the "fountain", alongside the Comares tower which contains the

Ambassadors' Salon dating from 1335, is a rigorously symmetrical structure. A large pool along its axis occupies almost the whole length of the courtyard, leaving free only the elegant porticos at each end. The second courtyard, the Court of the Lions, built between 1354 and 1391 by the king Mohammed V, presents a double symmetry, the two axes crossing at a stone fountain resting on the twelve fully-sculptured lions which have given the courtyard its name.

The Court of the Lions is entirely surrounded by a portico in which single and paired colonnettes alternate, and at each end of which stand delicate pavilions with pyramidal roofs, sheltering whispering fountains. Throughout, the raised and slightly-pointed arches rest on ornamented dies above colonnettes so slender as to seem unreal.

Throughout, the craft of chiselled stucco, traceries and scalloping all round the arcades in which the arches vary in their forms and the sharpness of their curve, the stalactites reduced to a honeycomb, all together form the delicate framework for an elaborate lifestyle.

What is most striking in this palace architecture, in contrast to the powerful masses of the Alhambra's double defensive wall, is its sense of fragility. The galleries of the porticos create a pleasant transition between the blinding brilliance of the sun on the light-coloured walls and the shade of the cool halls with their skilfully-worked ceilings. Like grottoes, octagonal star vaults glitter with a thousand facets. Ceramic mosaics brighten the tall dadoes with their high colour and irridescent reflections. Roofs of Roman tiles crown passages and halls.

These patios with their pools and fountains of splashing water, the tortuous passageways with spaces forever opening up and closing off in a game of ever-renewed surprises, these gardens of calm and complacent peacefulness, are the reflection of a dazzling civilisation in the last glow of its existence.

Near the Alhambra, the fountains among the rosebeds of the Generalife (Gennat-ou al-Harif, the Prince's Paradise) celebrate their oasis of peace in a kingdom at war, and which the final assaults of the Catholic Kings was to cast out of Europe in 1492, the same year—by a disturbing coincidence—as Christopher Columbus set off to find the Westward route to the Indies, and discovered America. It is on this fateful date that the Islamic epoque closes its book in Spain, and that the Reconquista, at the fulfilment of its mission, is to be transformed into a formidable imperialism to create one of the vastest empires in history.

Bottom:
The pool and porticoed pavilion of the Lady Tower in the Alhambra. With their lion fountains, these gardens demonstrate the refinement of the Nasrid court.

View along the Court of the Lions from inside a pavilion whose roof is supported on slim marble columns. Everywhere, water leaps and murmurs under the domes.

The magic of scalloped arches, delicately-worked stucco and abundant decoration: such is the dazzling spectacle of Nasrid architecture in Granada. This view from the back of a pavilion in the Court of the Lions gives a striking picture of the last brilliant spark of Moslem Spain.

The gardens of the Generalife in Granada, a veritable paradise where architecture blends with fontains and the rare scents of flowers.

The delicately stuccoed capitals and arches of the porticos around the Court of the Lions in the Alhambra. Here the Arab art of the fourteenth century has reached a summit of grace and lightness.

The star dome in the Hall of the Abencerrajes in the Alhambra, hung with stalactites: the art of delicately coloured stucco here gives the impression of an insubstantial shimmer of light.

Christian unity

The success of the Christians in putting an end to the presence of the Moors in Spain—a presence which had lasted seven hundred and eighty one years!—was due to exceptional circumstances: the kingdoms of Castile and Aragon, which had been through a series of bloody civil wars during the fifteenth century, had been reunited. Isabelle of Castile had conquered Aragon and married Ferdinand of Aragon; his coronation allowed the re-unification of the two Christian monarchies under the control of the Catholic Kings from 1479 on.

But the victory over the Moslems was accompanied by a new intolerance and fanaticism. First the expulsion or forced conversion of the Jews, and soon after that of the Moslems, despite the clauses in the treaty agreed when Granada capitulated. This led, through turbulent years that were to produce an intellectual impoverishment of the whole country, to a complete religious unification of the peninsula. This was a unification often enforced by the Holy Inquisition carried out by the Dominicans, a preaching order founded in the thirteenth century by the Castilian St. Dominic.

From the Conquistadors to the Baroque

After the discovery of the New World by the Genoese Christopher Columbus and his three caravelles sailing on behalf of the Catholic Kings, the history of modern times in Spain opens flamboyantly at the dawn of the sixteenth century with a succession of colonial conquests which were to give birth to one of the biggest empires ever to have existed. It was under the reign of Charles Quint (1516-1556) that the conquest and annihilation of the Aztec culture in Mexico took place, then the crushing of the Incas of Peru, followed in turn by the discovery of Chile and the establishment of a colony in Argentina.

From Charles Quint...

Charles Quint, who had been brought up in the Netherlands, rose to the Spanish throne under the name of Charles I, then in 1519 received the crown of the Holy Roman Empire in Germany from his grandfather Maximilian of Austria. He thus ruled simultaneously over the Netherlands, central Europe and northern Italy, and the kingdoms of

At Trujillo in Estremadura, Hernando Pizarro the Conquistador on his return from Peru had built his palace in the Plateresque style, sumptuously decorated with coats of arms. Younger brother of Francisco Pizarro, conqueror of the Inca empire, he had come home with his fortune made before leaving again for Lima, where he was killed by Almagro.

The Renaissance dome and Gothic lierne-ribbed ceiling of the cathedral in Cordova, built within the Umayyad mosque by the architect Hernan Ruiz in 1523.

Naples and Sicily. It was during this period, the first half of the sixteenth century, that Spain reached the apogee of its power and of the extent of its empire across the world. The gold of the two Americas soon flowed by the shipload into the peninsula. Coming in through Seville, which went through a period of great splendour, it produced an exceptional artistic outburst.

The Renaissance and the Plateresque style (so called because it was inspired by the style of contemporary silversmiths' work) gave birth to the most sumptuous buildings, benefitting from the great breath of the Italian Quatrocento, an influence that spread right across Europe.

The wealth and the well-rewarded aggressivity of the Spanish conquerors thus found expression also in their art. In 1523 the Chapter of Cordova decided on the construction of a cathedral, its design entrusted to the architect Hernan Ruiz. It was to be built in the heart of the beautiful hypostyle of the Umayyad mosque, which had already been transformed into a church. The mutilation perpetrated on this unique work created by generations of Moslem builders was quite irreparable. Not that Ruiz' work is in itself negligible: on the contrary it is an original synthesis of the last echoes of the Gothic, with lierne-ribbed vaulting, and the new classical forms. In this it constituted a renewal of the language of religious architecture, and it offers a sanctuary bathed in light where the sculptures and carved ornamentations stand out from their background in a clear atmosphere that overturned at one blow centuries of the Hispanic tradition. But for all that one would have preferred it elsewhere than in the middle of an Islamic monument.

Charles Quint repeated the same operation in Granada, at the centre of the Nasrid palace of the Alhambra, where he had built his own huge square palace. By this time Spain had thoroughly absorbed the lessons of Italy and brought back to life the classical styles: the palace's lower gallery is in the Doric order, the upper level is surrounded by Ionic columns.

...to Philip II

Charles Quint was succeeded by his son, Philip II. The German empire broke free of his control, then the Netherlands, but he retained a large part of Italy. He sought to reunite Spain, threatened by civil war and regional revolts, and he annexed Portugal. But the gold of the Americas was not always enough to quench the thirst for wealth: this infusion of gold from abroad, artificially swelling the treasury, stifled both agriculture and craftsmanship in Spain.

Shortly after transferring his capital from Valladolid to Madrid in 1561, Philip also decided to have built the palace-monastery of San Llorenç de l'Escorial. This magnificent and colossal work was entrusted to Juan Bautista de Toledo, but it was Juan de Herrera who completed it in 1584, while the building of the Pantheon was entrusted to Crescenti in about 1620. The palace lifts its severe silhouette in the harsh hilly countryside between the capital and Segovia; symbol of absolute power and of a proud world, it is laid out on an orthogonal plan expressive of a cold determination, a haughty grandeur tempered by the well-lit luxury of its apartments, sacristies and libraries, and by

The circular patio in the palace of Charles Quint in Granada, built in the mid-sixteenth century within the walls of the Alhambra.

Right:
The upper gallery of the Palace of Charles Quint in Granada. Luis Machuca's design is characterised by its elegant Ionic columns.

Facing page, top:
The west wing of the Escorial: this Renaissance palace-monastery, which Philip II ordered built by Juan Bautista of Toledo in 1561, is an imposing monument built to reflect the power of the Spanish empire.

Facing page, left:
The Pantheon of the Escorial was built around 1620 by the Italian architect Crescenti, in the basement of the monastery of San Lorenzo. Marble and bronze glint with a sombre and melancholy magnificence.

Facing page, right:
The dome over the crossing in the basilica of Escorial: a fine example of the severe Spanish Renaissance style.

the decor of the huge monastic basilica and sumptuous marbles of the royal Pantheon.

Philip was at war with England, who sought to rob him of the supremacy over the oceans of the globe he had won not only through far-off conquests but also through his brother Don Juan of Austria's victory at Lepanto against the Ottoman fleet. Now he built the "invincible armada"; 130 ships of the line and 30,000 men. But in 1588 these heavy vessels, caught in storms off the north coast of Britain, after being harassed by the smaller and much lighter English ships, were annihilated. It was the end of the Spanish navy, and from this point on the country was in decline.

The Baroque front of the Pilar at Saragossa.

Along the banks of the Ebro, the basilica of the Virgin of Pilar at Saragossa, built in 1681 on a design by Francisco Herrera the Younger. The huge building is 130 metres (140 yards) long and offers a forest of domes between four powerful corner towers.

The brilliance of Spanish baroque

This decline was indeed relative, for in the field of the arts, great names follow one on another, with El Greco in Toledo from 1575, Velasquez' career beginning in 1619, that of Zurbaran in 1629 and that of Murillo in 1646 in Seville. The seventeenth century was thus a golden age for Spanish painting. And with the church of Pilar at Saragossa, built by Francisco Herrera the Younger from 1681 and continued by Ventura Rodriguez, it was also the beginning of the Baroque style, which won much favour, as we know, throughout the Hispanic world.

In the eighteenth century Baroque was confirmed with the works of Churiguera at Salamanca. Then, under the influence of French art, and of the palace at Versailles which was imitated everywhere, Philip V had the delicious summer retreat of La Granja built to the south of Segovia. This palace is the work of a Spanish architect of German origin, Teodoro Ardemans, and the statuary that ornaments the front onto the park is signed by the French sculptor René Frémin.

It was also Philip V who called upon Juvara to built the Royal Palace in Madrid. The great architect died a year later in 1736, though not before he had designed a noble project. His successors Suchetti and Rodriguez were to cut down very considerably on the ambitious scale of the original project, but they nevertheless created in the Royal Palace a work not lacking in grandeur, and which, in its courtyard, is a fine example of the conjunction of Italian and Spanish forms.

By the time this palace was completed, Francisco Goya had begun his visionary career in Saragossa, announcing the upheavals of the Napoleonic adventure which shook Spain and all Europe at the dawn of the nineteenth century.

Such, very briefly sketched, is the story of Spanish art as it unfolded between the pre-historic era and the days of the Spanish empire.

The Palacio Real in Madrid, also built for Philip V, based on a previous design by Juvara. Building began in 1738, the year La Granja was completed.

Facing page, bottom:
The Palace of La Granja in Segovia, the front onto the gardens. Built for Philip V by Teodoro Ardemans between 1721 and 1739, it has been inspired by the Palace of Versailles.

95

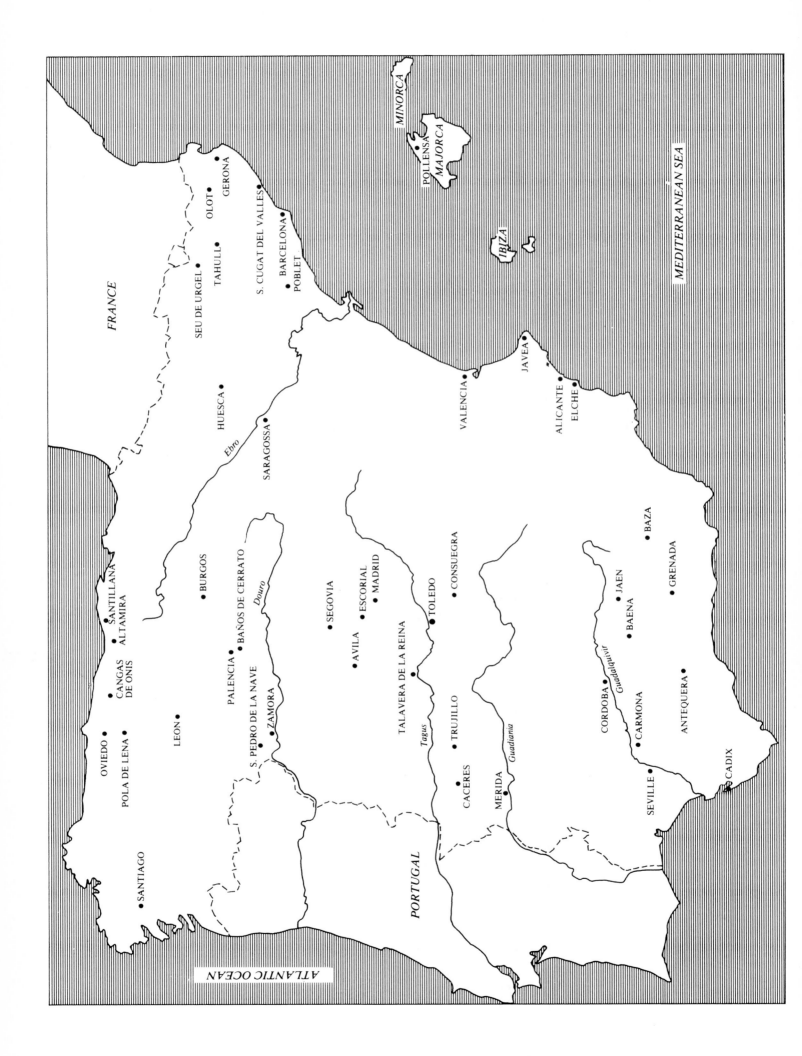

FRANCE

GERONA
OLOT
TAHULL
SEU DE URGEL
S. CUGAT DEL VALLES
BARCELONA
POBLET

HUESCA
SARAGOSSA
Ebro

MINORCA
MAJORCA
POLLENSA

IBIZA

MEDITERRANEAN SEA

JAVEA
VALENCIA
ALICANTE
ELCHE

BAZA
GRENADA
CONSUEGRA
JAEN
BAENA
Guadalquivir
CORDOBA
CARMONA
ANTEQUERA
SEVILLE
CADIX

BURGOS
SANTILLANA
ALTAMIRA
CANGAS
DE ONIS
OVIEDO
POLA DE LENA
LEON
PALENCIA
BAÑOS DE CERRATO
Douro
S. PEDRO DE LA NAVE
ZAMORA
SEGOVIA
ESCORIAL
MADRID
AVILA
TALAVERA DE LA REINA
TOLEDO
Tagus
TRUJILLO
CACERES
MERIDA
Guadiania

SANTIAGO

PORTUGAL

ATLANTIC OCEAN